THE BUGGY BOOK

CHAPTER 2

Electric Buggies

So you have decided to try your hand at a straightforward electric powered 1/10 scale buggy? What next?

Well, you will have a fair idea of the style of kit available from reading through the previous chapter, but let's take a closer look at the details of the buggy.

First of all, the styles of cars that buggies are modelled on are those used in such places as the Baja desert in the USA for racing. The most obvious thing about such cars is the type of tyre fitted, which is like nothing ever used on road cars. There is a range of tread tyres commonly found on such cars: a general purpose square "chunky" block pattern tyre, a spiked tyre most suited to grassy surfaces and finally a much smoother virtually tread-free sand tyre. As the wheels are out in the open with no mudguards, the wheels and tyres do dominate the appearance of the cars. The bodies are only rudimentary,

Tamiya racing buggies used Volkswagen-inspired trailing arm suspension.

Trailing link suspension on the 4-wheel drive Buggy.

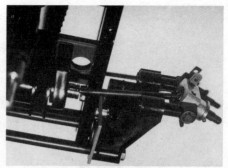

Double wishbone suspension of the Cross Racer *in close-up.*

enough to give the driver some basic protection from flying stones and something on which to fit the safety harness!

The first ¹⁄₁₀ scale buggies available, the Tamiya *Rough Rider* and *Sand Scorcher*, were scale models based on full-sized cars that used a large number of Volkswagen "Beetle" suspension parts and also employed a suspension system based on the VW trailing-link independent system at the front with swing-axle independent at the rear. This suspension system has proved, almost without exception, the best for 2-wheel drive cars, but for 4-wheel drive there are definite advantages to be gained from using the double, unequal-length wishbone style of suspension. At the rear end, both trailing arms and wishbones can be seen in addition to the early swing axle Tamiya system.

For suspension to work effectively,

The Holiday Buggy *is a good example of a moulded plastic "bathtub chassis" with shaped locations for components.*

A ladder-type chassis is used on the Tomahawk; note drive belt and pillars for body shell attachment.

the components need to be fitted to a rigid chassis, otherwise the chassis will tend to bend and flex, stopping the suspension from moving in the way that it was designed to. Chassis design has progressed from ultra-simple, flat glass reinforced plastic (G.R.P. or "Glass-Fibre") plates to highly complicated multi-component plastic moulded masterpieces. In between the flat G.R.P. plate and this design peak, there have been fully moulded "bathtub" types that hold all the component parts in cleverly moulded compartments and include all the fixing points for the suspension, motor, and R/C equipment, plus metal "ladder" style chassis with either roll cage "bodies" or plastic moulded body shells.

As well as simply holding the suspension, the chassis has to hold a motor, the nicad drive batteries and all

Tamiya drive system with first stage beneath a transparent plastic cover.

the R/C equipment and also provide solid fixing points for both tough bumpers and a body shell or roll cage.

Looking at the motor and drive system first, this will employ a single electric motor of either the 380 or 540 size. Although it is possible to use chains or belts (some buggies do indeed employ both somewhere in the drive system) the simplest of buggies use a gear drive from the motor to the rear wheels. It is not practical to use a single stage reduction gearing, as the rear wheels of a buggy are so large that if the gears are to have big enough teeth and they are to be of a sensible physical size, an extra intermediate stage of gearing is needed to allow the motor to turn at its most efficient speed. Most buggies will incorporate some means of altering the overall gear ratios so that the acceleration and top speed of the buggy can be matched to racing circuit requirements. Even though most of the parts of the gearbox will be of either soft, cast light alloy or plastic, there will be provisions for fitting either bearing-metal bushes or ball-races. A differential may be supplied as part of the kit. This device takes into account the fact that the outside wheel of a car travels further round a curve than the inside wheel and there will be more about it in later chapters.

With most forms of independent suspension there will be a need for some form of flexible or "universal" joint in the transmission of power from the motor to the rear wheels. This is necessary because the motor and gearbox are rigidly fixed to the main chassis of the buggy whilst the wheels must be free to move about and follow the undulations of the ground. There are

1. Mono-shock unit. 2. Wishbone. 3. Track rod. 4. Servo saver. 5. Steering servo. 6. Throttle servo. 7. Battery pack. 8. Speed controller. 9. Drive chain. 10. Drive shaft. 11. Gear cover. 12. Motor.

15

some buggies available where the whole motor, rear axle and gear box assembly pivots as a unit. This means that there are no universal joints in the system, which appears to be ideal because of its absolute simplicity. Unfortunately there are big limitations to this type of drive and suspension style, mainly because the "unsprung" weight is very high. If you think about it, the whole of the weight of the drive parts would be relying on the flexibility of the tyres to provide suspension. As there is so much weight in these parts, they do not follow the ups and downs of the rough surfaces too well.

Wheels, tyres, chassis, motor and suspension all form the "Rolling Chassis". To this are added control and power supply systems. Taking directional control, or steering, first, this function is carried out by a motorised device operated by the R/C system which is called a *servo*. This is coupled up to the actual steering linkage through a *servo saver*. The servo saver is fitted to prevent shock forces being transmitted from the wheels through to the small gearbox in the servo as it could be damaged in this way. The steering linkage follows full size automotive practice closely, in fact there are very few differences between the model system and full-size. Ball joints are fitted in various places to allow for full articulation of the steering and the Ackerman principles are incorporated to allow the wheel on the inside curve of a circle to turn a little tighter than the outside.

Steering is proportional, that is to say that the wheels on the buggy move as much or as little as the control stick or wheel on the R/C transmitter is moved. Of course simply steering the buggy is not enough: some form of control over speed is essential.

This can be done by several different types of controller ranging from a very simple two or three speed electromechanical device to a very sophisticated electronic unit that provides proportional forward and reverse control plus proportional braking and a power supply for the R/C equipment. As there is a full chapter on this topic elsewhere in the book, the only thing to mention within the context of this general description is that the electronic unit replaces a servo and, usually, the receiver battery. The alternative electromechanical or resistor controller needs a servo to drive it.

There are various types of nicad battery pack for buggies ranging from simple 5 or 6 cell packs held together by plastic sleeving to solidly boxed packs specially shaped to fit the battery compartment of particular buggies. The essential thing is that all the nicads used should be of the "Fast Charge" type, for the whole essence of the modern R/C electric model is the possibility of repeated operation at short intervals. Use of the incorrect type of battery is potentially very dangerous, as fast charging unsuitable cells can lead to an explosion.

To make best use of the fast charge capability, the battery pack is usually fitted with a quickly detachable mounting system and two-pin plug for fast charging.

If you wish to take fullest advantage of your R/C buggy you don't want to be limited to running it only on bright, dry, sunny days, nor do you want to be running something that is likely to be ruined by the slightest splash of water. To prevent damage from water and grit, or dust and mud come to that, there is likely to be fairly comprehensive protection for the R/C batteries and motor.

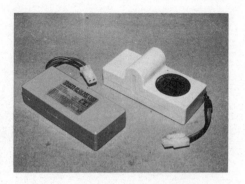

This tends to be more comprehensive on the lower cost, fun style buggies, since manufacturers seem to take the view that if you want to go racing you are prepared either to take the chance of wrecking your electronic equipment or spend more time devising a means of waterproofing of your own. By far the most common reason for skimping on waterproofing is to keep the weight down to racing rule minimum limits, as every extra gramme of weight the car carries cuts the performance.

Whether your chosen kit includes a full box to protect the equipment or just a couple of heavy duty rubber balloons to slip over the bits and pieces, the protection should really only be considered as "splash-proofing", not "water-proofing". There is a subtle distinction!

To top off the whole ensemble, there will be a roll cage or some form of body shell. Most racing rules include a requirement for a driver to be fitted, so you will always find that a little figure of some form is there. If you have a kit there will certainly be a range of self-adhesive decals ready for application to finish the whole thing off.

So much for a general description. There are of course a host of additions, variations and deviations – oil-filled dampers, adjustable servo savers and anti-roll bars to mention only three!

Full protection is offered by a radio crate as used on this Beetle, at the cost of a little extra weight.

CHAPTER 3

Internal Combustion Buggies

For all intents and purposes, there is only one size of engine used and one scale of I.C. (internal combustion) engined buggy available for serious buyers – ⅛ scale, powered by 0.21cu.in. (3.5 cc cubic capacity) glowplug motors. There are a very few kits to be found for ¹⁄₁₀ scale I.C. buggies, but they are not used at all for competition in the U.K. or Europe. The engine size for ¹⁄₁₀ scale is 0.10 cu.in (2.00 cc), incidentally.

The development of ⅛ scale buggies has not followed quite the same path as that of the smaller electric powered vehicles. By and large, ⅛ scale I.C. buggies have never been the true scale models that the electric world has seen, but instead much more functional chassis designs have been coupled to a wide variety of suspension designs. Those buggies produced in the Far East have almost exclusively incorporated "trailing arm" style suspension while the European models have favoured "twin wishbone" suspension.

To be fair, from many points of view the trailing arm layout is a superior suspension system, but for the more powerful, faster and heavier ⅛ buggy, the problems of keeping drive shafts in place and also building pivots strong enough has proved to be more trouble than the benefits warrant.

Four-wheel drive systems also found early favour with ⅛ scale buggy designers. The handling benefits were very soon appreciated and with the power available from the modern glowplug motors, the additional weight and frictional losses in the drive system did not seem to be worth considering.

British-made Irvine 20 ABC car engine has tall cooling-fin head.

Results have proved this to be the case, for although two-wheel drive buggies are fast in a straight line and can be made to handle very well round corners, the 4-wheel drive machine is so much easier to drive that whereas the 2-wheel buggy driver is on the limit of concentration when driving fast, the ease with which the 4-wheel drive buggy can be controlled and small mistakes can be corrected mean that the 4-wheel drive always comes out the winner at the top levels of competition.

Control of ⅛ scale buggies is by the same two-function radio control system that is used for the electric machine. Because the model is bigger and heavier, there is a tendency for the actuating devices for steering and throttle to be larger and more robust and consequently more power is consumed by the R/C system, demanding the use of re-chargeable nicad batteries.

MECHANICAL DETAILS
So much for the broad concept of ⅛ scale R/C buggies. The actual machine has many similarities to its electric counterpart, but there are obviously

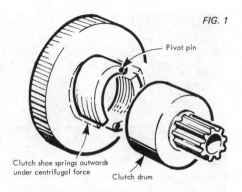

FIG. 1

Pivot pin

Clutch shoe springs outwards under centrifugal force

Clutch drum

striking differences. Chassis styles can be said to echo precisely those of the electric models but the power plant, drive train and ancillaries are very different.

Accepting that the buggy has an engine, the first requirement is for a means of being able to stop the buggy moving without stopping the engine. Starting the engine, although fairly simple, is not something that one would wish to do following every halt in the forward progress of the buggy! A centrifugal clutch is fitted that engages as the engine speeds up and automatically

One of the first 4-wheel drive I.C. buggies was from Kyosho of Japan. Chain drive to front and rear.

19

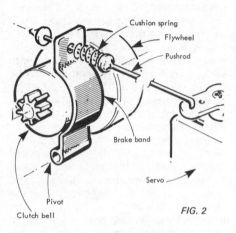

Cushion spring

Flywheel

Pushrod

Brake band

Servo

Pivot

Clutch bell

FIG. 2

disengages when the engine is slowed. (See Fig. 1). As the buggy would free-wheel with the throttle closed and the clutch disengaged and as it is quite heavy, a brake is fitted. This can be a very simple band brake that rubs on the clutch drum or a more sophisticated disc brake with either single or multiple discs. Some buggies may even have more than one disc brake unit. (See Fig. 2)

An engine uses fuel and this needs to be carried in a suitable sized tank in an accessible place so that it can be refilled without too much difficulty. The standard size tank for competition purposes is 124cc and it would be usual to find a tank of this size supplied with a kit model. Between fuel tank and engine there should be a filter to clean the fuel before it reaches the very small orifices of the carburettor. Even if fuel is filtered before putting into the bottle or whatever is used actually to fill the tank, there is a danger of grit finding its way into the fuel because of the nature of the sites on which buggies are operated.

Finally, there needs to be a silencer for the engine. This is absolutely vital. *Never run a buggy engine without a proper silencer fitted* and if the silencer comes off whilst the buggy is running, stop, and repair it immediately. Running without a silencer will not harm the

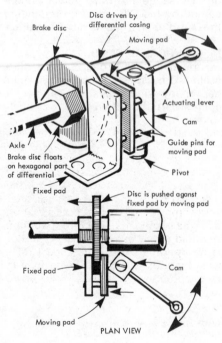

Disc driven by differential casing

Brake disc

Moving pad

Actuating lever

Cam

Guide pins for moving pad

Pivot

Axle

Brake disc floats on hexagonal part of differential

Fixed pad

Disc is pushed aganst fixed pad by moving pad

Fixed pad

Cam

Moving pad

PLAN VIEW

engine or the buggy, but will certainly harm your relationships with anyone who happens to live anywhere near you and could also damage relationships for other more considerate buggy drivers too!

Some kits are supplied with silencers as standard, others simply leave it to the purchaser to find and fit as best he can something suitable. It is strongly recommended that the newcomer to the sport only considers a kit that has adequate parts and instructions included for a proper silencing system. Some kits even go so far as to supply a "universal" manifold to couple up the silencer to the engine, but this is far from common. The more usual situation is for the engine manufacturer to offer a manifold either as an inclusive item or as an optional extra. This aspect of ⅛ scale buggies is covered more fully in the chapter on engines later in the book.

A typical silencer (muffler) unit. Silicon tube connects sections.

POWER TRAIN

So much for the actual power-producing section of the buggy. The drive has now got to be transmitted from the engine to the wheels, either all four (4WD) or just two of them (2WD).

There are four different ways of taking the drive from the clutch to the wheels: gears, chain, belt or shaft. To deal with these in order:

Gears. Normally pure gear drive systems are only found on 2WD buggies. Quite simply, the cost of building a

gearbox to drive from front to rear of the 4WD buggy would be unrealistic, it would be too heavy and have too many parts to go wrong. Often gear drive is seen on buggies with engines that are mounted with their crankshafts running fore and aft, when bevel or contrate gearing is needed to turn the drive through 90°. The major benefit of this arrangement is that the engine can usually be started by simple direct application of an R/C aircraft type cone starter on the end of the crankshaft. Bevel gears can be expensive to replace, so it is as well to make sure that gears are really carefully meshed so that they don't strip.

The bevel gear set-up is often coupled with a toothed belt drive from the engine to a layshaft, although this first stage of reduction may be by spur gears. Braking can either be on the layshaft or on the main axle. This style of car is favoured by the Japanese manufacturers and is available from most. Extensive use is often made of light alloy die-castings in the drive train.

These do provide excellent protection for the gears but can be vulnerable to abuse, both from overtightening of screws during assembly and crash damage. The cast cases are next to impossible to repair if broken so just in case, do make sure that the buggy you choose is backed up by a good spares service.

It is also worth noting that this type of transmission style lends itself to standard rotary barrel throttle equipped engines; slide carburettors are more difficult to fit.

Chains. These usually form a second stage in a drive system. It is usual to fit a gear stage from clutch to layshaft followed by the chain which can be used to take drive to just two or to all four wheels.

For really efficient power transmission and low wear rate, the chain should be proper roller chain having free-running rollers on each link. Unhappily this is not always the case with 4WD chain drives. Most 2WD chains are

The gear drive on this Mantua car is accessible from the rear and the pinion carries an extension for use with a cone-type starter.

CHAPTER 4

Kit Assembly

Electric and I.C. engine powered buggies are indisputably different, but there are many similarities between them from the point of view of building up kits. This chapter should be read by all would-be buggy drivers in conjunction with the more specialised chapters on specific aspects of buggies. For example, for more detailed information on mounting engines refer to Chapter 7, whilst Chapter 9 provides hints and tips on assembling dampers. Wherever necessary, the differing techniques for I.C. and electric power buggies will be emphasised.

A TOOL KIT IS ESSENTIAL
Although most kits for buggies do contain the necessary hexagon wrenches (Allen keys) you will certainly need some other tools. Many kits make the proud boast that "only a screwdriver is needed", and this will not be an idle claim. If a screwdriver is needed, make certain that it is a good one that you use! If necessary invest in a new, good

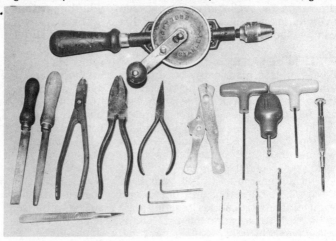

Typical tool requirements for buggy building. The wire stripper, centre right, is not essential but is convenient.

quality Phillips or Posidrive type and a couple of good standard type screwdrivers.

As well as screwdrivers you will need pliers; 6 to 8in engineers' "combination" pliers and 6in. "snipe nosed" will do. A small tack hammer and a model makers' vice are useful, plus a modelling knife, scissors, soldering equipment, a hand drill and a range of small twist drills suitable for drilling metal.

A PLACE OF YOUR OWN

A well-lit place of work and a solid table with a work surface that will not be damaged by the assembly processes are next on the list, plus a supply of small containers to hold all the various screws, gears and so on during building. It will be found that most kits package similar parts together, thus meaning that many small packets have to be opened simultaneously to put together just one sub-assembly.

If you cannot have a permanent workshop to carry out your buggy building and subsequent maintenance, then try to arrange for a good sized empty drawer to be available and then keep everything on a suitable workboard that can be placed bodily inside the drawer.

IF ALL ELSE FAILS!

Please, please read instructions before you start even to open the packets in the kit box. One well-respected American R/C car kit manufacturer starts off the instruction booklet for his model by stating that – "You can build this car without reading the instructions, good luck, you'll need it if you do!"

Even if the model is not your first, there will be numerous little details and even minor modifications that may need to be made to parts that the instructions will cover which you will never know

about otherwise. In a lot of cases the order of assembly is critical in certain components: change the order and you can waste a lot of time taking things to pieces because you have taken something a stage too far without appreciating the need to fit a vital part at a particular point.

WILL IT COME UNDONE?

One major problem area for the complete beginner to buggy building is that of things falling to pieces when the buggy is run. It seems impossible to tighten the screws properly and no matter how tight you make them, in minutes they are undone again.

Once the buggy is first assembled, you have probably set the pattern for evermore. If parts are not properly assembled first time round, then the inevitable wear as they start to loosen spoils fits of parts and they just won't hold together in the future. Threadlocking compound is only part of the answer. In the right place it is invaluable, but in the wrong place you may live to regret using it as you try to dismantle your buggy for servicing.

The first key to success is having the proper tools for the job and the next is developing a sympathy with the materials and fixing devices and methods used. The latter does not grow overnight but is acquired over a period of months and years. There are a few basic rules that can help speed up the process of gaining experience.

Take a look at the different types of screws used, for a start. There are steel screws with slotted or cross-point heads and "cap" heads with hexagonal (Hex.) sockets for Allen keys; there are Hex. socket grub screws and Hex. socket countersunk head screws. Almost without exception, these Hex. socket screws will be high tensile steel and very strong. They are also reasonably hard and providing that the Allen keys used with them fit well, there is little likelihood of them being damaged. As a general rule there are two ways of using an Allen key: if the short end is inserted in the screw then a lot of leverage can be obtained and vice-versa if the long end is inserted. Use the maximum leverage mode for socket cap screws into steel and the minimum leverage mode for all small grub screws and any screws into light alloy or plastic mouldings. (See Fig. 5)

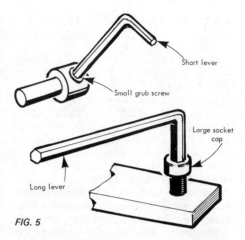

FIG. 5

With both standard slotted screws and Phillips or Posidrive screws, make certain that you are using the correct and appropriate size driver. Take a look at the shaft of the screwdriver and choose one with a diameter no greater than the diameter of the head of the screw. The blade should fit the slot exactly. Beware of tightening screws while holding parts in your hand – one slip and the screwdriver is in the palm of your hand. Place parts on the bench before applying pressure. Apply pressure as you turn the screwdriver to make sure it doesn't slip from the slot.

Don't use pliers for doing up nuts. A small adjustable spanner is just acceptable if it is a really good quality one, but ideally small spanners or sockets should be used.

Thread-locking compounds are available in a whole range of different types, some of which are now thought of as "permanent" methods of assembly. In other words, they are not intended to be used on anything that is to be taken apart for maintenance. Don't use this variety. Nor should you use thread-locking compound on plastic to plastic or plastic to metal joints unless you are certain you know exactly what the plastics are and you are certain that the thread-lock you are using will not attack those plastics.

In general I would avoid using thread-lock on very small grub screws unless it is of a very soft nature and in any case would only use thread-lock in a place that I can apply heat to with a gas blow-lamp so that it can be softened to ease dismantling. Never use cyanoacrylate

Engine retaining bolts are one case for thread-locking compound.

FIG. 6

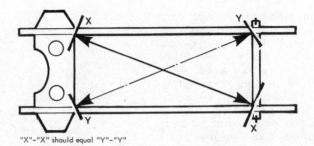

"X"–"X" should equal "Y"–"Y"

glue (Super Glue) to lock threads and never use thread-lock on an engine crankshaft. Two of the prime reasons for pieces coming apart are that either they did not mate together properly before bolts or screws were fitted or the wrong length screw was fitted and could not therefore be screwed properly home. Do make certain that all burrs and swarf have been properly cleaned from parts and that you have correctly identified the screws for the job in hand.

CHASSIS ASSEMBLY
First and foremost a chassis should be stiff and without twist. If your buggy chassis is a fully moulded plastic or pre-assembled type then there is little you can do to influence these factors. Many kits need the chassis assembling, however, and the accuracy of this operation will dictate the quality of handling of your buggy. Twin rail chassis are most critical in this respect. The fixing screws should firstly be done up loosely, then the complete chassis put down on a solid flat surface and pressed down firmly whilst the screws are finally tightened. These screws are definitely a case for thread-lock. The same technique should be adopted wherever possible with any multi-part chassis. Check the diagonals of rail chassis after assembly to ensure that they have not parallelogrammed.

SUSPENSION PARTS
To make sure that the suspension does its job properly it is particularly important that the pivots are free moving. Try out the fit of the parts without any springs, anti-roll bars, steering or dampers fitted. The suspension should flop up and down to its full extent of travel as the buggy is turned over. If this is not the case trace the source of the stiffness and treat it before proceeding any further. Holes moulded into plastic parts can vary in size slightly because of tiny variations in the temperature of the molten plastic during the moulding process. Ideally the holes should be finished to size with a reamer. This is a precision cutting tool (and expensive) and in most instances only a drill will be available to open out holes. Do not use a round file, the result of which will be a barrel-shaped hole that will wear very rapidly. Only when you are sure that the suspension is fully free should you move on to the next stage.

BEARINGS
There are three types of bearing found in buggies, plain bearings or bushes which can be either plastic or metal, usually bronze, ball bearings, which may be sealed, open journal and thrust type, and "Torrington" roller bearings, often found in clutches.

Reaming wishbone holes with reamer held in a tap-wrench.

The enemy of any bearing is dirt and the buggy is generally operating in the worst possible environment for this. Wherever possible sealed ball races should be fitted. Unsealed bearings are quite suitable for use inside gearboxes, however. Ball-races require very little lubrication, in fact too much of the wrong lubricant will speed up wear rather than cut it down. Use a really good quality oil and soak the bearings in it; it is not a good idea simply to squirt oil at the outside of the bearing in between races. For one thing hardly any will actually get into the bearing and for another it may well carry dirt into the bearing and will certainly cause it to stick all over the outside of the bearing.

With plain bearings we have a "Catch 22" situation. Without oil the friction is too high, with oil dirt sticks all over the bearing area. The best solution here is to clean wheel spindles before each run and apply a small quantity of oil. In this way there will be a minimum of grit on the bearings at all times. A penetrating aerosol chain lubricant seems very good for ball-races; there are various brands available and a good car accessory shop is the place to go for this.

Bearings must be fitted with care, particularly if they have to be pressed into housings. Use the spindle which the bearing is to carry as a guide to help here and if possible press in with a vice rather than use any sort of impact from a block of wood or a hammer. (See Fig. 8) Bearings can often be helped into metal housings if the housing is warmed up in a domestic oven first. 200°C should be hot enough.

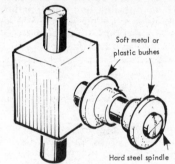

Soft metal or plastic bushes

Hard steel spindle

Ball-race bearing

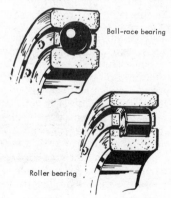

Roller bearing

FIG. 7

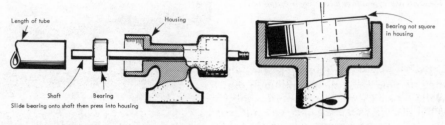

Length of tube

Housing

Bearing not square in housing

Shaft   Bearing

Slide bearing onto shaft then press into housing

FIG. 8

RUNNING CLEARANCES

When assembling moving parts one aspect that is frequently neglected is end float, that is to say endways movement. (See Fig. 9) Excessive end float will rapidly wear the side faces of gears and even the teeth of bevel gears, so wherever possible use thin washers to pack between moving parts to cut down this movement. End float is particularly important on drive shafts and on the suspension arms of buggies that have trailing arm type suspension. When drive shafts are fitted first move the suspension to full travel in each direction and check for a small working clearance for the drive shafts — say ½mm. If this is present at the extremes, now see that it is there throughout the suspension travel. Make this check with the wheel hubs pressed firmly inwards towards the centre of the car. You are looking for the "worst possible case". Is there a small amount of clearance present when everything is pushed up

close? Now check the opposite extreme, can the drive shaft fall out when everything is pulled apart as far as it can go?

If the clearance is excessive in the minimum clearance situation then it will need to be taken up with small packing pieces inside the drive cups on the output shafts from the gearbox. If you have a damaged spiked tyre, cut off a spike and trim this to suit. On four-wheel drive buggies these checks are further complicated by the need to make sure that the clearances are correct as the wheels steer as well as while the suspension moves up and down. A particular point to watch is play in suspension joints. Tremendous forces are applied to the suspension arms as the buggy drives round and it is necessary to pull and push really firmly on suspension parts while making these checks. Finally, on four-wheel drive buggies fit any packing pieces to the inboard or gearbox end of the drive shafts, as fitting them at the outboard

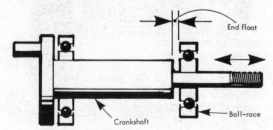

End float

Ball-race

FIG. 9   Crankshaft

Drive shafts and spacers to reduce end float.

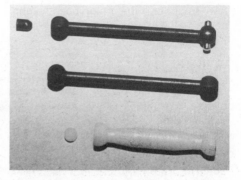

ends will put the pivot points of steering and drive shafts out of alignment and generate excessive feedback loads through the steering.

TYRE FITTING

Some buggies make it easy for the builder when it comes to tyre fitting, providing a clamping system of some form that does not require the builder to glue the tyre on to the wheel. If this is the case, read no further, if not read on!

In spite of the glib comments in instruction books it is rare for either the materials of tyre and wheel to be suitable or the fit of tyre to be close enough for simple glueing to hold tyres adequately. By far the best system yet devised involves purchasing a cycle tyre inner tube which is then cut into lengths to slip over the wheel hub. The chosen inner tube must be a tight fit. Roughen up the plastic wheel hub and coat with a non-thixotropic contact glue and also apply to the inside of the inner tube. When this is dry, apply another coat to the wheel hub and while it is wet slide the tube over it.

The tube will now be very solidly fixed to the plastic hub and the actual buggy tyre can now be fitted over the hub and cyanoacrylate glue (Super Glue) used to fix it. The reason for adopting this method is that cyano glue does not seem to adhere well to plastic hubs and impact glue does not adhere well to tyres. However, cyano bonds

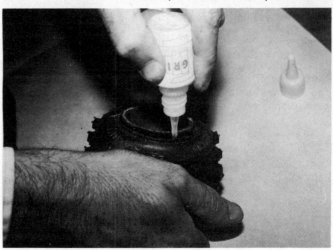

The last stage of a tyre-fitting sequence, glueing the tyre to a rubber sleeve on the hub with cyano-acrylate.

tyre to inner tube magnificently and contact glue likewise secures inner tube to hub! Simple, isn't it?

RUNNING-IN

Don't be too impatient to rush out and race a brand new buggy around before giving it a careful check under close observation. If it is electric, then the motor should be run in before being subjected to full power. This can be done while the buggy is under construction. Hook the motor up to a two-thirds discharged nicad or, even better, only two cells instead of the full five or six. Allow the motor to run without any load for several hours, stopping it every now and then to lubricate the motor and gearbox bearings. Once this process has been gone through there should be a noticeable improvement in the smoothness and freedom of the gear-box and drive train. There are alternative and even quicker methods of running in electric motors but for a new buggy this system has the dual attraction of running in buggy and motor alike.

An I.C. buggy should be given the same treatment. Start up the motor, then put the buggy up on blocks and allow the motor to run for a while, meanwhile noting any mechanical problem. This also gives a chance for final adjustments to be made to the carburettor before the buggy is driven. Don't be tempted to rev the motor up to full power whilst the buggy is off the ground. There is a chance that the engine will not withstand the resulting RPM! You may also find that the tyres come off the hubs at extremes of RPM. When you are quite happy about the reliability of the whole mechanics of the buggy then take it for a spin.

CHAPTER 5

Radio Equipment

Radio control (R/C) equipment has already been briefly mentioned but to help get the best from it, a much fuller explanation is really necessary. By and large, it is immaterial whether the equipment is to be used for electric power or I.C. engine buggies, but where there are differences they will be pointed out.

Two-function equipment is the type generally fitted, but although there are only two functions required for full control, there is no reason why R/C outfits with more than two functions should not be used. The two functions are for control of direction and speed. For an I.C. powered buggy, cleverly devised linkages enable the two functions to be used for brakes as well as throttle.

Although there is absolutely no need for the user of the equipment to understand how it works, a little understanding does help. The R/C system is made up of a transmitter, a receiver, servos and a power supply for the receiver. Transmitters for R/C are a reasonably familiar sight these days and most people will have seen an example of these "Black Boxes" at some time. The "Black Box" has in some instances been superseded by more suitable purpose-designed buggy transmitters which look more like futuristic weapons. Traditional transmitters have two control sticks on the front face, arranged with the stick for throttle control on the left, that for steering on the right. Pistol style transmitters use a wheel for steering, again operated by the right hand, and a trigger for throttle control. It is possible to find traditional-shape transmitters fitted with wheel style steering, but

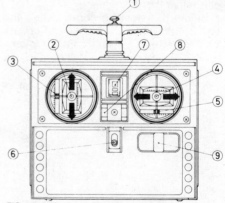

FIG. 10 1. Aerial. 2. Throttle control stick. 3. Throttle trim lever. 4. Steering control stick. 5. Steering trim lever. 6. On/Off switch. 7. Battery state indicator. 8. Fixing for neck strap. 9. Interchangeable crystal.

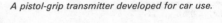

These are called trim levers and can be used to correct a bias to the steering of the buggy so that it runs straight "hands-off".

There will also be a meter of some sort, which may be either a battery state meter or a measure of the actual output of the transmitter, and there will be an aerial which will be telescopic. (See Fig. 10) Many transmitters incorporate additional features and these will all be described later in this chapter.

The transmitter serves to send the control information in a coded form as a radio wave to the receiver. This is how it does it.

Modern R/C equipment is "proportional", that is to say that if you wish the steering of your buggy to move a little bit, you move the stick a little bit, and so on. The servo, the actual "muscle" of the R/C system, moves just as far as you wish, precisely following the tiniest movement of the transmitter control stick. An encoder within the transmitter generates three pulses, one for each of the control sticks plus a third known as the reset or synchronisation pulse. The

these are not very common now. Both control sticks are fitted with springs to centralise them.

Below the steering control stick and to the right of the throttle stick there are two additional small control levers.

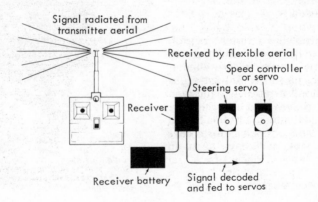

FIG. 11

Standard two-function transmitter, with car-borne equipment.

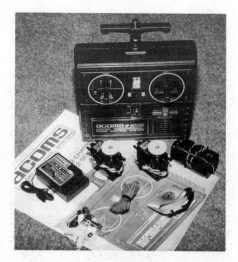

control sticks vary the length of the transmitted pulses which are transmitted repeatedly in a set order — throttle, steering then reset.

Inside the receiver, there is a decoder which sorts out the pulses and sends them to the appropriate servo. Firstly when the receiver is switched on, the decoder waits until it recognises a reset pulse. As soon as it has found a reset pulse it knows that the next pulse it receives must be sent to the throttle servo, the next to the steering and then reset etc. (See Fig. 11)

Inside the servo there is further electronic circuitry which can convert the varying length of the pulse it receives into an instruction that tells it where it is supposed to be. What happens is that the servo generates a pulse of its own, a reference pulse. It compares this with the length of the pulse sent to it by the receiver and if it is a different length it knows that it must drive until the pulses are the same length. This is a continuous process which results in the servos smoothly following the control stick or wheel movements. (See Fig. 12)

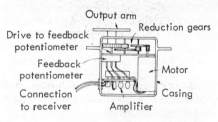

FIG. 12

POWER SUPPLIES

Most transmitters have a battery box with a removable lid. Either six or eight pen-cell batteries will be fitted and these can be either dry batteries or rechargeable nicad (Nickel-Cadmium) batteries. More expensive equipment will probably have nicad batteries fitted as standard and may not have a battery box that is easily accessible. Receiver

Receiver internals. Stepped end is for servo and battery plugs.

Examples of servos. Arms can be used instead of discs for output.

battery packs can also be either dry or rechargeable, dry cell sets having battery boxes that will readily accept rechargeable cells. With receiver battery boxes, the easy-change facility is a two-edged sword. If the batteries are easy to fit, they can also slip out easily, and it is a very good idea to wind a rubber band round the battery box to keep the cells in place. With any form of battery box it is important that the cells make good contact with the terminals of the box. Keep contacts clean and bend out the springs from time to time to maintain contact.

Most R/C manufacturers recommend that alkaline cells are used for both transmitter and receiver. These are expensive and for receiver power packs, on I.C. buggies in particular, do not last very long, as little as two or three hours of use. Once a couple of sets of these batteries have been used beginners usually realise the false economy of dry-cell equipment. Although nicad cells are more expensive initially, they can be recharged many hundreds of times at virtually nil cost. It is quite possible to replace directly the dry cells with nicad cells, since although the nominal voltage of the nicads (1.2 volts) is lower than that of the dry cells (1.5 volts) this small difference will not affect the performance of the equipment.

A means of charging the nicads is of course needed. If you purchase the R/C equipment manufacturer's conversion kit, there will certainly be a charger available. If not, then the easiest solution is to buy a charger and two battery boxes for charging. Then, to charge the cells take them out of the equipment and place them in the boxes, charge up and re-fit. Charge time is dependent on the output of the charger. It is best to buy a slow charger for transmitter and receiver which will fully charge the batteries overnight, around 14 hours for

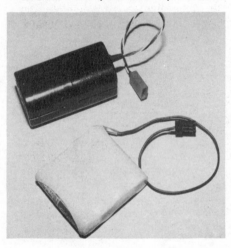

Two types of nicad packs for receivers, flat and square.

Battery stowage in a transmitter: may be nicads or dry cells.

a full charge. This type of charger will not damage the batteries if they are left on charge for too long occasionally. Once the batteries have been fully charged once, that is when they are first purchased, a charge of 12 hours maximum is sufficient unless they are inadvertently allowed to go completely flat by, for example, being left switched on overnight. As a rough guide, for each hour of use charge for two hours plus ½ hour for each day the equipment has stood idle up to the recommended maximum.

There has been a tendency recently for even dry-cell equipment to make provision for fitting rechargeable cells, a socket being fitted for charging. It is thus not necessary to remove the cells from the transmitter for charging. Such transmitters sometimes also arrange for the voltage to be nearer the same for both dry-cell and rechargeable operation by fitting a spacer into the battery box so that only seven dry cells can be fitted.

ADDITIONAL FEATURES

Although there are quite a few sets sold that only have the absolute basic specification, this being the age of the microchip, there is a growing tendency for more and more extras to be fitted. First on the list is *servo reverse*. It will be appreciated that if the steering is considered, if the control stick is moved to the right, then the servo could move either to the right or to the left depending on the way the system is set

up. If the servo rotates say clockwise and the steering moves the wrong way, then the facility to reverse the servo is obviously very useful. This feature may be fitted to just the steering or may be fitted to both controls.

Next comes *rate control*. Under normal circumstances buggy drivers will set the steering linkages so that the steering moves as far as possible to give maximum control. When it is wet, however, this may well be too much steering throw, so an adjustable throw or rate is a desirable feature. It can also help to be able to cut down throttle throw on I.C. buggies in wet conditions.

Charging cells with a simple two-output mains plug charger.

41

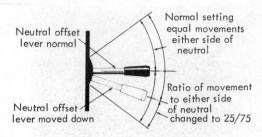

Neutral offset lever normal

Normal setting equal movements either side of neutral

Ratio of movement to either side of neutral changed to 25/75

Neutral offset lever moved down

FIG. 13

Two controls operate the dual rate or, as it is sometimes called, ATV (Adjustable Travel Volume), a switch to switch the facility in or out and an adjustment potentiometer – a "volume control", if you like – to vary the amount by which the servo throw is reduced. These controls are normally fully accessible from the front fascia of the transmitter. A small screwdriver will normally be needed to make adjustments if the R/C system was designed initially for R/C aircraft use; model aircraft fliers don't like the controls to be inadvertently moved, so such adjustments as trims are made a little more difficult to operate. On buggy systems, there will probably be an adjustment knob fitted. In use the buggy would be driven round, any requirement for adjustment noted and the model pulled into the side of the track while the alteration was made and the procedure repeated until the set-up was as required. Then, if at any time more steering was felt to be necessary, the switch could be clicked over for extra throw.

It is quite possible that however well the steering is set up on a new buggy, once it is placed on the track it will be found to turn more sharply to one side than to the other. Assuming that everything else on the buggy is as it should be, this would be a case for an indepen-

dent *end point* adjustment facility. With this adjustment, it is possible to set the travel of the servo either side of neutral independently. Just two potentiometers provide this facility, and they may be either inside the transmitter or fully accessible from the outside of the case.

On many buggy R/C systems there is an extra lever to the side of the throttle stick, opposite the trim lever. This can be used to off-set mechanically the throttle control stick neutral point (see Fig. 13) which gives the servo used for either throttle or speed controller operation more travel to one side than the other. This is a useful facility, as often the speed controller requires this arrangement and it can be difficult to achieve if the servo travel is symmetrical. On I.C. buggies, the throttle almost always needs more travel than the brakes, so once again the *off-set neutral* is very useful.

Exponential rate is frequently included on buggy transmitters, but this facility is not widely used nor widely understood! Best described as a "soft neutral", exponential rate varies the rate of servo response to stick movement. A large movement is needed around the neutral point to attain a specific servo movement, getting progressively more even in response towards the extremities of travel. If a buggy has particularly sensitive steering in a straight line then there may be a case for trying out the exponential facility so that full cornering power is retained whilst de-sensitising the buggy on the straight.

There are new developments turning up on R/C equipment continuously, but don't be put off a set because it has one facility missing. Many drivers have all the above gadgetry and may never use any of it! In the actual race it is your skill

at using throttle, brakes, steering and reverse on a well set-up car that will bring success. The technology may make it easier to set the car up but you will still have to drive it well.

LOOK AFTER IT PROPERLY

It would not be true to say that the R/C gear takes as much maintenance as the buggy, but it cannot just be thrown into a corner time after time following use and be expected to give of its best. There are a few tasks that should be a regular part of the maintenance schedule after every driving session, basically comprising cleaning and making a few simple checks.

Even if you drive an electric buggy indoors, perspiration and dust will combine to produce a build-up of muck on the transmitter case. Clean the outside of the transmitter with a detergent and damp cloth. Don't splash the whole thing in water unless it is unavoidable. If you do get it wet put it into a warm dry place until it has properly dried out; an airing cupboard is ideal.

Pull the aerial right out then carefully clean the sections with a tissue or cloth dampened with methylated spirits. While you are doing this you can check for any damage to the aerial. This item has to carry the high voltage, low current signals and needs good contact between each and every section. If there is any damage, get a new aerial — they are not expensive and a faulty aerial can cause immense frustration, not to say damage to buggies.

I would recommend that you obtain an aerosol of switch cleaner/lubricant to clean such items as charging sockets and servo output sockets. This can be obtained at electronics shops. Do not use aerosol products containing WD40 on electronic circuitry, particularly near the transmitting sections, as it has been known to cause problems.

Once the transmitter is clean, turn to the receiver, which should be removed from any protective covering used. It is surprising how much condensation will often be found inside the waterproofing. If this is not dried out then the electronics will surely suffer. A dry airing cupboard is once again an ideal place for this. Once it is all perfectly dry, clean the servos and their leads, the switch harness and all plugs and sockets with the aerosol contact cleaner. Check the receiver aerial for any signs of damage and you are ready to reassemble the equipment for a check-out.

This check-out is important for it may well be that the poor handling you experienced during the last minute or two of your final run was not just because of the tyre you found was coming off, but because the servo output gear was stripped! Plug everything in and switch on. Move the control sticks very slowly and deliberately so that you can observe the servo travel. Any hesitation or jerkiness is a sign that there is something wrong. The servo should travel from one end of its travel to the other with no variation in smoothness. A broken gear is usually indicated by the servo motor audibly whirring with no corresponding movement of the servo output arm. I would not recommend the inexperienced to try to repair a servo, if you suspect damage, return the servo to the equipment supplier for qualified repair.

Now, charge up the batteries if the set has rechargeable batteries, or remove dry cells if they are fitted. Properly looked after, a modern set of R/C equipment will give many seasons' use before it needs replacing. It is a very good idea to send it to the manufacturer's service agent once a year for tuning, however. You may not be having any problems at all with your gear but if it has drifted out of tune it may well be "splattering" interference on to the channels alongside your own. Hardly fair to save a few pounds on servicing your equipment at the expense of others is it? When you do send equipment back for servicing make sure that if it is nicad powered the nicads are properly charged and that you have removed any non-standard plugs or other connectors. You will be sure to be charged by the servicing agents for returning the equipment to standard specification if you have changed anything round. The reason is quite simple – all the agents' test equipment will be designed to connect to standard gear and unless yours is to standard specification, they cannot check it out.

R/C INSTALLATION

Electric buggy builders are likely to have an easier time of R/C installation than most I.C. buggy builders. Quite why this should be is not clear, but perhaps the manufacturers think of electric buggies as being for beginners, which is not a fair assumption really.

Any guide to installation is likely to be just that, a guide. There are so many minor variations between one set of R/C gear and another that fittings that are too specific are not too helpful, unless of course you had the specific equipment catered for! Positions of component parts are frequently critical and should not be changed unless there is a very sound reason. Even then, don't burn your boats by sawing, filing or generally cutting away material, you might regret this when you realise that there was a good reason for siting the switch where it was shown in the instructions.

Servos should be fixed on resilient mountings. Don't be tempted to dispense with the rubber grommets to make steering more positive, since this will shorten the life of the servos. Particularly on an I.C. power buggy, the receiver and battery pack should be suspended on rubber bands. (See Fig. 14) A more solid fixing can be used on an electric buggy but only if a softer fixing is impossible. While fitting the receiver and battery pack, consider waterproofing. Heavy gauge balloons are one of the best things to use. Suitable types are often available from specialist model shops. Slip the balloon over the component, then secure the neck with a tightly twisted rubber band or small plastic tie-wrap. Try to mount the component so that the neck of the balloon faces to the rear. The switch can also be covered with a piece of balloon trapped between switch and mounting to keep it in place.

Specially made heavy duty servo arms are available for buggy use, suitable for most makes of servo. Particu-

FIG. 14

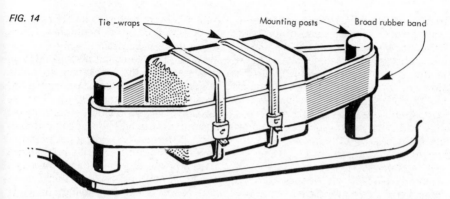

Tie -wraps   Mounting posts   Broad rubber band

larly for steering try to use these, as the loads on the servo will distort the normal types supplied with the gear. Linkages from the servo to servo saver, throttle or speed controller should be as rigid and direct as possible. Connections to the servo saver and to the servo disc should be at 90° to avoid unwanted "differential" coming in, which is particularly important with the steering. (See Fig. 15) As supplied some ball-joints are very stiff, but if it is possible to use some form of captive joint for the steering they can be made very free moving without fear of them dropping off at awkward moments. To size them,

spin the ball parts of the joints in the chuck of a drill and polish them with fine emery cloth.

Make sure that the steering and throttle do not lock up at their full travel position before the servo has reached the end of its travel. Move the control stick slowly and smoothly and watch very carefully to see that the steering continues to move to the full extent of trim travel.

Throttle and brake operation from a single servo puzzles many people, but it is not difficult to grasp. There is a simple system of over-ride springs so that from neutral the servo opens the

FIG. 15

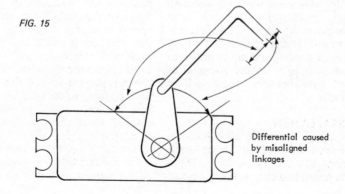

Differential caused by misaligned linkages

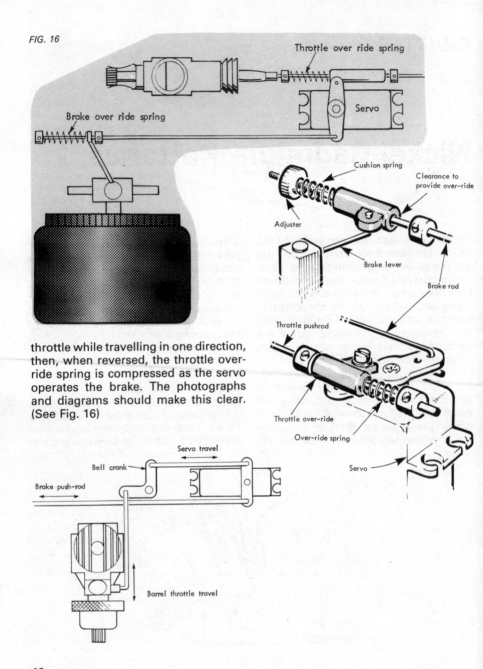

FIG. 16

Throttle over ride spring

Brake over ride spring

Servo

Cushion spring

Clearance to provide over-ride

Adjuster

Brake lever

Brake rod

Throttle pushrod

Throttle over-ride

Over-ride spring

Servo

throttle while travelling in one direction, then, when reversed, the throttle override spring is compressed as the servo operates the brake. The photographs and diagrams should make this clear. (See Fig. 16)

Servo travel

Bell crank

Brake push-rod

Barrel throttle travel

46

CHAPTER 6

Nickel-Cadmium Batteries

Fast charge nicad batteries were the key factor that made it possible for R/C electric power buggies to develop. Prior to the arrival of these batteries, either very expensive silver-zinc or slow to charge lead-acid batteries were the only thing readily available. Coupled with the fast-charge characteristic, these nicads can be fast discharged, important for really good performance.

There are a number of terms that will be used throughout this chapter in relation to nicad batteries, and these need explanation before we start.

Cell: a single nicad "Battery".

Battery: several cells joined together in series.

Series: method of electrical coupling of cells. Individual cells are connected in a string positive (+ve) to negative (−ve) to give a battery pack voltage equal to the sum of the cells i.e. 6 cells = 6 × 1.2 = 7.2 volts. (See Fig. 17)

Parallel: alternative method of coupling cells, side by side with all +ves together, all −ves together to multiply capacity. (See Fig. 17)

Voltage: electrical "pressure", for nicad cells nominally 1.2 volts.

Capacity: storage ability, usually expressed as the number of Amperes (Amps) that the cell can deliver in a stated time i.e. Ampere/Hours (AH) or may be expressed in Milliampere Hours

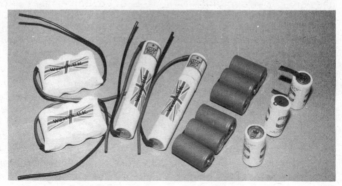

Various arrangements of nicad battery packs, with individual cells at right. Each pack contains three cells in series.

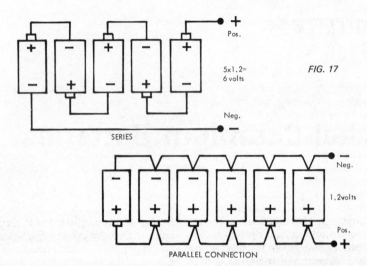

5x1.2=
6 volts

FIG. 17

Pos.

Neg.

SERIES

Neg.

1.2volts

Pos.

PARALLEL CONNECTION

(mAH). The capacity chosen for buggy use is 1.2 AH or 1200mAH, there being 1000 Milliamps to 1 Amp.

The terms Ni-Cd or nicad are convenient abbreviations for nickel and cadmium, the two metals that are used to make the cell. Nicad cells are alkaline, that is to say that they employ an alkaline electrolyte, not an acid electrolyte as found in the more commonly recognised lead-acid cell. This should in any event be called a lead-carbon cell, with the additional information that it uses an acid electrolyte!

Neither of the metals is actually present in solid slab form: they are sintered or deposited on to carriers. The sintering process involves a powdered metal being heated up until it fuses, resulting in a porous structure that for a given weight of material gives a very large surface area on which the electrochemical reactions can take place. It is because of the large area of cell plate produced by the sintering process that the cell has such a large capacity for giving out current. The electrolyte is usually soaked into a fibrous separator which is placed between the metal parts of the cell, the resulting "sandwich" being then coiled like a swiss roll and placed in a sealed container.

The distinguishing characteristic of the fast charge nicad as compared with its slow charge counterpart is that it is "vented". This means that instead of the chemical reactions of the cell process going on in a hermetically sealed can there is a pressure release or safety valve fitted. This is needed because in extreme cases of overcharging the cell is unable to re-absorb the gases generated during charging sufficiently quickly and pressure starts to build up inside the cell. The cell case could explode unless it was fitted with a release valve or vent.

If the cell is overcharged to the point where the vent actually comes into operation, the cell will be permanently damaged. Many vents are in fact single operation devices that do not re-seal; once they have vented the cell should be thrown away. While the cell remains sealed and is charged and discharged within its design limits, the chemical balance within the case remains constant. Over-charge and vent the cell and some electrolyte will escape in the form of hydrogen gas. There will be a reduced amount of electrolyte left in the cell, so the next time the cell is charged it will not hold its charge so well. Attempts to put more charge into it to bring it back up to its previous level may well cause it to vent again, and so on.

For buggy use cells are arranged in 5, 6 or 7 cell packs in series with nominal voltages of 6, 7.2 or 8.4 volts. The highest voltage is that decided upon for International competition and as it is a rather special case, will be dealt with separately. At one time the capacity was stipulated as 1.2AH for competition purposes and thus most suppliers found it necessary to follow this ruling. However, as the nicad battery manufacturers vied with one another to produce better and better cells for the price, a good selling point was 1.4AH capacity in a 1.2AH casing!

This presented difficulties for the racing fraternity, so they decided to adopt the more sensible approach of specifying the cells by physical size without mentioning capacity, for this latter form of control had obviously become unrealistic. The chosen size is the internationally recognised "Sub-C" which is a nominally 1.2AH cell but, as described above, can be 1.4AH or almost anything!

TYPES OF CHARGER
Many buggies are sold initially with a mains operated charger, which will be of the slow or trickle charge type and frustrating to use, for the batteries will take at least 12 hours to recharge. For full use to be made of the fast charge

possibilities the following equipment will be needed.

a) A fast charger. There are many of these available ranging from the simplest "Dropping Resistor" to very sophisticated "Automatic Pulse" chargers. Each type will be dealt with in detail.

b) A current source for charging from. A 12 volt lead-acid car battery is the usual thing to use.

c) A charger for the lead-acid battery, usually a mains-operated trickle charger.

d) Alternatively, you can buy a mains electricity operated fast charger but this cannot be used away from a mains supply, a distinct disadvantage if you wish to take your buggy to an outdoor race meeting.

In general terms the more foolproof the charger, the more it will cost. Charging batteries is however not simply a matter of connecting up the battery to a charger and then leaving the charger to get on with the task. Well, not quite, anyway. To get the most from

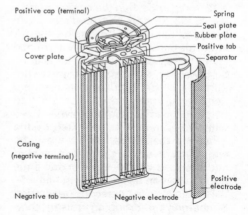

FIG. 18 Reproduced courtesy Sanyo Marubeni (U.K.) Ltd.

your cells you will need to understand them and treat them properly. So, although it is the simplest, and most probably the system that can most easily go wrong, if you are seeking top performance then a simple dropping resistor or at least a range of different value dropping resistors will work well.

The "dropping" principle is common to all the chargers, for if the nicad battery was to be connected directly to a 12 volt source then the charge current would be far too high and the nicad would be damaged. A dropping resistor limits the current flow to pre-determined levels by resisting the flow. This is quite hard work so the resistor gets very hot during its efforts! Dropping resistors need to be mounted on heat sinks to help them radiate the heat away. Even with the current flow restricted by the dropping resistance, all is not total simplicity, for unless the charge is timed and stopped at the appropriate time, the battery can easily be overcharged.

This leads on to the second generation of charger, the dropping resistor combined with a clockwork timer. This represents a big improvement over the simple resistor. At least, come what may, the battery can never be charged for more than 20 minutes! This can still lead to overcharge, however, if the battery is not completely discharged before connecting up.

One of the big advantages of the nicad is its very flat discharge curve. If we were to plot a graph of cell voltage against time we would see that the nicad voltage drops quickly for the first few seconds then remains nearly constant. Shortly before it is fully discharged there is another rapid voltage drop. (See Fig. 19) This is great for running the model, as performance stays at a uniform level throughout the running time of the buggy, but not so good when it comes to charging. It is not possible to measure the voltage of the cell and with any reliability predict the state of charge of the cell.

To combat this problem electronic engineers have taken careful note of some other characteristics of the nicad, the cell voltage whilst the cell is on charge in particular. They noted that the cell voltage rises quite rapidly as the cell approaches a fully charged state and then drops immediately the cell is charged. A type of automatic charger known as a "Peak Detection" charger which can monitor the cell voltage and switch off the charging current is the result. With this type of charger, it doesn't matter what state of charge the battery is in when the charger is coupled up, as when it is fully charged, whether 30 seconds or 20 minutes later, the electronics can cope and safely and automatically stop the charge. If you add to the charger the facilities to recognise for itself when it is coupled up incorrectly and refuse to function until corrected, and also to double as a Digital Volt Meter (D.V.M.) and in some cases an Ammeter as well, then you will realise that such chargers, although expensive, are probably the best route to follow for the enthusiastic buggy driver.

CHARGING TECHNIQUES

The foregoing description of the different chargers available will have set the scene on charging. It should already be clear what the various techniques are in principle but some additional clarification would do no harm.

If you decide to opt for the very simplest form of dropping resistor for your charging you will need in the initial stage a 25 watt 1 ohm resistor and either a commercially produced heatsink or a piece of sheet metal (aluminium) on which to mount it. You will also need suitable connectors for your nicads and 12 volt source. With this equipment only attempt to charge fully

discharged cells and then for a fixed time of 20 minutes. Make sure the cells are fully discharged by running your buggy until the power drops off dramatically. As a general principle, allow cells to cool before recharging.

If you have gone one stage further and wish to use a charger with a clockwork timer, then exactly the same rules concerning discharging and charging time apply.

There is an intermediate stage between the simple dropping resistor and the fully automatic system, indeed some would reckon it to be the ultimate method, and this demands a stepped charging technique coupled with a peak detection system.

For this you will need a ½ ohm resistor and heatsink as well as the 1 ohm resistor. The idea is to charge the battery in steps starting off with 5 minutes using the ½ ohm dropper, then changing to 1 ohm, then monitoring the voltage of the cells for the peak voltage while the cells top up using both resistors in parallel. This and other such

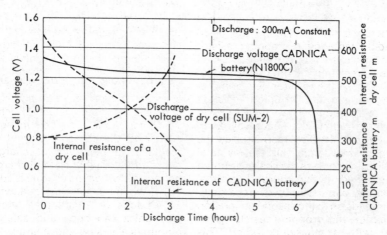

FIG. 19 Reproduced by courtesy of Sanyo-Marubeni (U.K.) Ltd.

The Cord Auto fast charger is as near foolproof as possible.

systems are all very well for the very experienced but are fraught with dangers for the beginner.

Whichever method you choose to adopt, the cells will benefit if they are properly discharged and kept cool before and during charging. To discharge the cells it is not enough just to couple up a load, either a motor or electric light bulb, to the cells. They really must be discharged as individual cells. This is not easy, particularly if you have a

buggy that uses one of the nicely boxed battery packs. If you are really serious you will be well advised to remove the cells from the plastic box and sleeve them in heat shrink tubing. This has the dual benefit of lowering the weight and improving the heat dissipation from the cells. If you already have shrink wrapped cells then it is simply a matter of cutting small "windows" in the plastic tubing at the cell junctions so that a probe can be inserted to make contact with the cells and terminals. You will need a good voltmeter – a digital type is to be preferred – and a load of some sort. Some buggy drivers use a very cheap 0-10 amp meter as the load, since this can also be used for other current-measuring purposes. In practice the cells are individually discharged to a level of 1.1 volts, and this is an important figure; most authorities recommend that the cells should not be taken below this figure otherwise they can be permanently damaged.

The theory is that if all the cells are discharged as a pack, there could be some cells that finish up below 1.1 volts and some that finish up well above the 1.1 figure, although the average voltage is 1.1. By regular individual discharging you can be certain that the cells are being taken to a common charge level and also that none is being taken to a lower level that could cause the higher voltage cells to feed back into the lower. As the cell are joined in series, this could reverse the polarity of these cells.

High temperatures are to be avoided in nicad cells. If the cells start to warm

Multiple outlet mains charger can be used for R/C or drive batteries.

Accessory box containing charger, with built-in cooling fan.

up during charging it is a sign that the charge rate is too high or that they are being overcharged. Do not allow the cells to become more than slightly warm to the touch, any higher and you should stop charging straight away. Before charging either allow plenty of time for the cells to cool down or cool them with a fan, cool box and ice-packs or even, in extreme cases, put them in a bucket of water. During charging a cooling fan should be used for best results. It is also worth remembering that electrical conductivity goes down as temperature goes up, so a cool cell will give more current than a hot one.

BATTERY PACK ASSEMBLY

Most buggy drivers will be content to buy ready-made-up battery packs for the first buggy but at some stage may wish to make up a special shaped pack or use some individually purchased cells. First of all make certain that the cells purchased are suitable for the job. They must be fast charge, vented cells with spot welded tags fitted. It is not a good idea to try to solder directly onto the cell canister. Quite simply this will cause local heating inside the cell and this can permanently damage the cell.

You will need a 25 watt soldering iron, electrical resin in cored solder, suitable hook up wire, a connector compatible with your buggy and correct sized heat shrink tubing. Virtually all buggies take battery packs in the form of "double sticks", that is, two sticks of three end-to-end joined cells arranged in side by side configuration. Assem-

bling this type of pack is a two stage operation. Firstly solder the cells in two sticks of three cells, joining them +ve to –ve (series connection). Now slide a length of heat shrink tube over the stick and apply heat to shrink. A hair drier usually does the job. The two sticks can now be laid side by side and either joined up using "super glue" or a hot melt glue gun. The pack can now be totally sleeved with more heat shrink

Soldering of cells needs to be neat and quick to avoid damage.

53

tube or just be reinforced at the ends. Fit the chosen connector, making certain that the wires to it from the cells are of adequate size to carry the current and that they are well supported so that continual plugging and unplugging of the pack does not break the solder joint. Last of all cut the tiny windows in the wrapping for the access to the cell junctions needed for discharging purposes.

CARE AND CAUTION

Nicad batteries are remarkably tough things and a certain degree of abuse can be heaped upon them without apparent ill effect. There will be hidden effects, however, probably slight reductions in capacity, a shorter life, or poorer discharge rates, all factors that affect the performance of your buggy. Take care of your batteries and you will be rewarded with better performance. There are a few "Don'ts" that should be remembered:

DON'T overcharge.

DON'T overheat.

DON'T over-discharge.

NEVER charge in a sealed R/C crate that contains a speed controller. If the cell vents and gives off hydrogen gas, when the speed controller is operated a spark could cause an explosion.

BEWARE of short circuits. A shorted-out pack can give out incredibly high currents and at the first sign of a short circuit (heat, smoke etc. from the battery pack) cut through the wiring that joins the cells to break the connections immediately. It is more important that the circuit is broken than that your buggy cannot be raced again on the day! If a short does occur beware of the high temperature and fire danger.

BUGGY MOTORS

All of the buggies currently available are provided with a motor as part of the kit. This will fall into the class of motor that is known as a "Standard" motor. This is again a racing class term, for the racing classes are separated only by motor specification and most manufacturers like to supply a buggy that is suitable for racing. The second class of motor is known as "Modified", once again in line with the Modified racing class.

The motors used are three pole direct current permanent magnet motors using ceramic magnets.

STANDARD MOTORS

A "Standard" motor is made to a specification laid out in the buggy racing rules. This specification is roughly as follows—

a) Motors are subject to a maximum price limit (£10 at the time of going to press).

b) Only certain specified motors can be used (Igorashi, Mabuchi and Yokomo).

c) They must be unopened, in other words they must not have been taken apart and no modifications can be made by the purchaser.

Various motors are available that fall into this specification, and most of them will have similar performance. After all, they are not very expensive and the amount of work the manufacturer can afford to put into them is limited by cost.

A Standard motor is the very best choice for a beginner to buggy driving. Although the appeal of the higher power Modified motor is obvious, using it to best advantage needs experience. In fact, the beginner will probably find his buggy is faster on a standard motor than with a modified.

MODIFIED MOTORS

Really modified motors are rarely that at all, they are bought as complete ready to use items. The term "modified" really stems from the racing rules once again, as these allow buggy racers to modify the motors that they buy. Commercially available modified motors are again subject to a price limit (£35 currently) but may be uprated by the addition of ball-races, better fitting of parts, more precise balancing and various other tuning "tweaks". Most important of these tweaks is the "wind" of the armature. This refers to the number of turns of wire and its thickness which sets the character of the motor. The thicker the wire, the more current the motor will draw and the more power it will produce. Remember, though, that the more current the motor draws, the less time it will run for on a charge, although expert modifications made to motors can improve their efficiency quite a lot, making it quite possible for the buggy to go faster and keep going for just as long.

CHAPTER 7

Engines and Accessories

Engines used to power buggies are almost without exception two-strokes. For those unfamiliar with internal combustion engine principles, a brief description of the way these engines work will be a great help to long term usage.

The two-stroke engine is a very simple device, it has three moving parts:

a) Piston – this moves up and down in a cylinder, pushed by the force of expanding gases in the combustion chamber.

b) Crankshaft – this converts the reciprocating movement of the piston moving up and down the cylinder to a rotary motion.

c) Connecting Rod – connects the piston to the crankshaft.

Other parts of the engine are:

a) Crankcase – encloses all the reciprocating and rotating parts and includes provision for mounting the engine either in the form of lugs or a base mount. Also usually includes provision for mounting a carburettor and exhaust system.

b) Cylinder Liner – tubular sleeve in which the piston fits, closed at the top by the Cylinder Head to form a Combustion Chamber.

c) Backplate – seals the rear opening of the crankcase (See Fig. 20).

In operation the two-stroke is very simple. A mixture of fuel and air is drawn into the crankcase via the port or opening in the crankshaft. This happens because as the piston slides up the cylinder, pressure is lowered in the crankcase, thus causing atmospheric pressure to push air through the carburettor, picking up fuel as it does so.

As the piston starts its return journey down the cylinder, the crankshaft valve closes and pressure starts to build up in the crankcase. As this happens, passages called transfer ports open up between the lower part of the crankcase and the combustion chamber.

Fuel and air mixture now transfer to the combustion area. Next time the piston goes up, there will be fuel and air mixture in the top of the cylinder which will be compressed. (Note that also more fuel is being drawn into the crankcase to continue the cycle)

Once the piston gets to the top of the cylinder, the compressed fuel and air mixture is ignited, whereupon it burns fiercely, the heat of combustion causing expansion of the gases, which drives the piston down. The descending piston simultaneously drives the next charge of fuel and air to the combustion chamber. Finally, as the piston nears the bottom, the exhaust port is opened and the expanded gases are allowed to escape.

To summarise – as the piston goes up, it compresses and draws in fuel and air, as it goes down it produces power and transfers fuel and air mixture from crankcase to the cylinder.

Somewhat simplified, but if you have now grasped these basic operating principles, further descriptions of the tuned pipe, tuning-up and fault finding will be that much easier.

IGNITION AND FUEL

The term "ignition", or at least reference to the fuel being ignited, has already been made, but without any specific indication being made as to how this is done. The most familiar method of igniting the fuel/air mixture compressed in the cylinder of an engine is the sparking plug. Certainly, this method of ignition has many advantages and may find a place in buggies in the future, but the system used for model two-strokes is most commonly glow-plug ignition. The use of the glow-plug is confined to a class of engines referred to as Semi-Diesels, that is to say that they don't compress the fuel/air mixture enough for the heat generated by compression to cause unaided ignition, nor do they need quite such a high temperature igniter as a spark. Instead, the semi-diesel uses a glowing element fitted

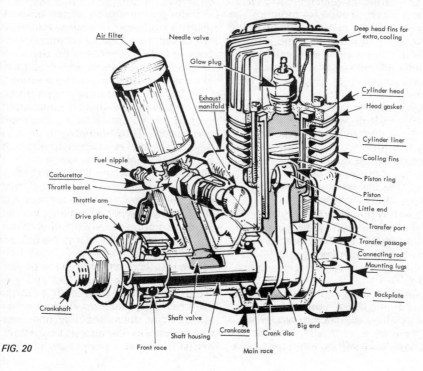

FIG. 20

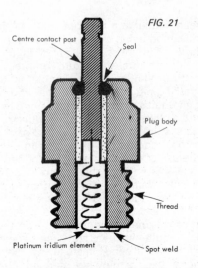

FIG. 21

Centre contact post

Seal

Plug body

Thread

Platinum iridium element

Spot weld

into the combustion chamber to provide the extra heat needed for ignition. The glowing element is contained in a little device called a glow-plug and is a tiny coil of platinum alloy wire. Platinum is chosen because of its ability to act as a catalyst giving out heat when surrounded by the fuel/air mixture. This heat is insufficient on its own to ignite the mixture from cold so the element is further heated by passing an electric current through it during the starting operation. Once the engine is running, then the "booster" battery used to cause the element to glow can be disconnected. A combination of the catalytic reaction between platinum and fuel/air mix and general heat inside the engine keeps the element hot from one "burn" to the next (See Fig. 21).

FUEL AND OIL
Fuel used for buggy glow-plug engines is based on alcohol. Methyl Alcohol or "Methanol" is the chosen type; this is not the same as Methylated Spirits ("Ethanol"). As will be appreciated, the fast-moving parts inside an engine require constant lubrication. As the whole of the inside of a two-stroke engine is constantly bathed in fuel, how better than to carry the lubricating oil to the moving parts in the fuel? This is just what is done. A suitable proportion of oil is mixed with the methanol and the engine runs on a basic mixture of 4 parts methanol to 1 part oil. It is not possible to mix ordinary mineral oil with methanol (the sort of oil used in the family car) but a vegetable oil mixes well and castor oil is the usual type. Castor oil is a particularly good lubricant at the high temperatures found inside a glow-plug engine. In fact the temperature needed to stop the oil doing its job would probably melt the inside of the engine!

There are other oils that can be used, nearly all of them synthetic types which are chemically engineered and do not occur naturally. Synthetic oils have remarkably good lubricating properties and can be used in much lower proportions than either of the natural products, as low as 1 part oil to 10 of methanol.

Such oils sound ideal but there are some snags. They are not as tolerant to high temperatures as the natural oils. If the engine is allowed to overheat, the oil can break down and stop lubricating the moving parts. The result of this happening is seizure. The engine stops suddenly as the parts bind together, an expensive occurrence. To help prevent this happening accidentally, many fuels contain a small percentage of castor oil as well as the synthetic used as the principal lubricant.

Even if you do not intend to go racing, it is best to own and run an engine that starts easily, runs smoothly and ticks over reliably. In the height of summer and with a brand new engine this is possible with an engine running on "straight" methanol and oil fuel. However, this is an ideal condition and reality is more like a partly worn motor and a cold day! There is no doubt at all that the addition of nitro-methane to the fuel can help bring about all the benefits mentioned above. Nitro-methane, or "nitro" for short, is very expensive: the cost of 10 litres of nitro equate to the price of a reasonably good glow engine!

Fortunately you do not need a great deal of nitro added to the fuel to bring about a big improvement in performance. A minimum of 5 per cent is recommended. Because the addition of nitro produces a power gain of almost 1 per cent power for each 1 per cent nitro added to the fuel, racing buggy drivers have been known to add up to 50 per cent to their fuels. For most purposes 10 per cent will be entirely adequate, although 20 per cent would be a good figure for racing.

There are several other chemicals that are claimed to be "nitro equivalents", such as nitro-propane and nitro-ethane. They do work to some extent but, particularly, the latter is to be avoided as it causes a big increase in operating temperatures. Try to make sure that your fuel contains genuine nitro-methane.

BUYING YOUR ENGINE

So much for the basics of the engines and their fuel. At some stage you will be forced to take the plunge and choose which engine to buy. Even with something as essentially simple as a glow-plug engine there is a range of possible types within the general classification. Firstly it must be understood that an engine must be fitted with a ball-race mounted crankshaft. The side loads placed on the shaft really demand this;

a plain bearing shaft would only last a short time.

In fact there are no true "buggy" class engines with plain bearings, nor true "car" engines, come to that. It would be possible to economise falsely by purchasing a plain bearing "aircraft" engine and fitting the necessary extra cooling fins to it and thus convert it. The main differences between engines in the buggy class involve the piston cylinder material and construction. The very simplest engines use a cast iron piston running in a very accurately finished steel cylinder. This style of engine is cheapest to make and although performance is little different to the next grade up, that is "ringed" piston motors, the wear rate is higher and it is more expensive to bring the engine back up to as-new performance.

Ringed piston motors use steel cylinders and aluminium pistons fitted with a cast iron piston ring. As can be seen, the actual materials that run together are steel and cast iron in both cases, but in the case of the ringed piston, only a very narrow ring of cast iron contacts the cylinder. Also the principle of the ring is that gases from the burning fuel/air mixture squeeze their way behind

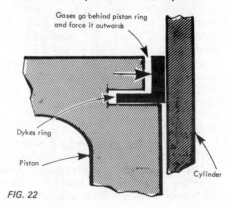

FIG. 22

the ring and push it out to press against the inside of the cylinder, thus giving a closer fit and better performance. A worn ring can also be easily and cheaply replaced without the expense of replacing the whole of the piston/cylinder assembly (See Fig. 22).

One of the main problems of producing close fits in these engines is the fact that the heat inside the engine causes the parts to expand. As there are different materials used in the engines they expand at different rates and unless the materials are chosen carefully, the engine will either seize up or become so slack that there will be insufficient compression for it to run properly. The ringed piston gets over this problem by using a springy piston ring with the actual piston a slack fit, whereas the lapped piston motor relies on very accurate fits during initial manufacture.

If it were possible to produce a really close fitting piston/cylinder assembly that expanded just the right amount to give an optimum fit at full operating temperature, yet still lasted a reasonable time without any penalties of high

frictional losses, that would be just what was required. This aim involved quite a few years of hard development work before it was evolved into a practical proposition in the form of the A.B.C. piston/cylinder. The abbreviation stands for Aluminium, Brass, Chrome and the principles of operation are as follows:

a) Aluminium piston is light in weight, a desirable feature as heavy pistons strain connecting rods and crankshafts and make it difficult to balance-out vibrations in the engine. Careful choice of exact composition of the piston alloy matches the expansion to the brass cylinder.

b) Brass cylinder is well matched to the aluminium for expansion, easy to make and chromium plate.

c) Chromium plated cylinder. The plain aluminium piston would soon wear out if fitted into the best finished normal cylinder. Chromium plate provides a very hard and very smooth low friction surface for the piston to rub against.

There are several variants on the basic A.B.C. theme, such as nickel plating instead of chrome (A.B.N.) or aluminium cylinders in place of the brass (A.A.C.). The latter frequently dispenses with a separate cylinder liner, the piston running straight inside a chromium or nickel plated crankcase. Both of these variations are attempts to produce equivalent performance at more acceptable costs, both nickel and aluminium being cheaper than chrome and brass.

The very best of racing buggy motors all fall into the plated cylinder classifica-

Pico 'Buggy' engine developed especially for ⅛ buggies.

tion and the choice really lies between this type of motor and the ringed piston motor. Few plain lapped piston motors are now available for the buggy driver. Having decided on the price range of the motors that can be considered, next you will have to turn to your chosen buggy and check out the availability of such items as clutches, engine mounting blocks, carburettors and exhaust manifolds. Not every manufacturer makes a suitable fitting for every engine available and you may have to modify your choice to suit the ancillaries available.

CLUTCH FITTING

There are several different types and styles of clutch available, they can be grouped as follows:

a) Universal clutches, which often have spring loaded shoes and theoretically need no modification to suit any engine. Such clutches usually fit onto the crankshaft, retaining the propellor driver still frequently supplied with R/C car engines. While they usually work well if properly set up and maintained, these clutches are often inferior to those supplied by the larger circuit car kit manufacturers. (See Fig. 23).

b) Aluminium flywheel bolt-on clutches, usually with PTFE (Poly Tetra Fluoro Ethylene) shoes, collet fixing. These generally need the crankshaft trimming for fitting. (See Fig. 24).

c) Clamp-on clutches for which all the threaded section of the crankshaft is removed, the flywheel gripping the plain ground section of the crankshaft. (See Fig. 25).

It is first necessary to check that the thread in the clutch supplied fits the engine you have chosen. The two common sizes are ¼in UNF or 6mm with the straight unthreaded sections of the shafts 6, 6.5mm or ¼in diameter.

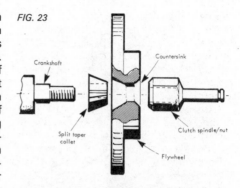

FIG. 23

With many clutches it is necessary to press the shoe pivot pins into the flywheel. This operation is simple enough if you have a vice available. Don't use a

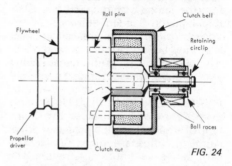

FIG. 24

hammer, find someone to do the job for you with a vice. Most pins are pushed through from the rear of the flywheel, particularly if they are of the solid type with knurled ends to make them a tighter fit. Do not press them through

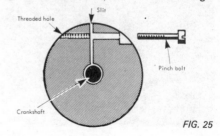

FIG. 25

FIG. 26

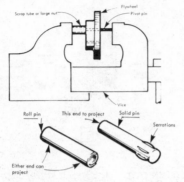

the flywheel any further than is necessary, as if you do the ends will probably foul the inside of the clutch bell when this is fitted. (See Fig. 26).

When the pins are pressed in check that they are square to the face of the flywheel. If not, a gentle tweak with a pair of pliers will set things to rights.

FITTING UNIVERSAL CLUTCHES

Even if the clutch is designed to fit any type of engine using the propellor driver supplied with the engine, a little extra care can save future frustration. The smooth rear face of the flywheel needs to be roughened up a little for reliable drive action. I use a centre punch to make a roughened area and then apply thread-locking compound to the mating

surfaces. You must check that the engine crankshaft thread does not bottom out in the clutch nut. It may be necessary to trim a few millimetres off the end of the crankshaft. Most shafts are at least surface hardened and a few (O.S. for example) are hardened all the way through. The best tool for trimming is a low voltage power tool with a grinding disc. Be very careful: you must fully protect the engine from any abrasive particles and also wear safety spectacles. I put the engine inside a polythene bag with just the end of the shaft protruding from a hole in the corner.

Don't under any circumstances allow any metal particles to get into the engine, since this will destroy it in no time flat. Wrap the end of the shaft in masking tape and mark the length to be cut off. Grip the section that is to be thrown away in a vice and slowly cut through the shaft. Don't allow the engine to fall onto the floor as the cut is completed!

There may be a burr to remove after this cutting operation. Grind this away and tease away any excess on the start of the thread with a hard and sharp tool.

The flywheel can now be bolted onto the engine. I have never found it necessary to use any form of thread-locking compound and would strongly advise against its use. If the thread is cut to the correct length and the nut is done up properly then it isn't needed. Tighten the clutch nut finger tight then with soft jaws in the vice, grip the flywheel and with a correctly fitting spanner do up the clutch nut. Experience has to be the guide here; a torque wrench could be

Pressing pivot pins into a flywheel using a bench vice.

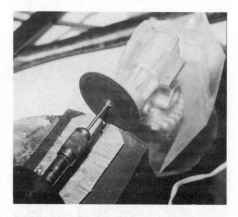

Cutting away surplus crankshaft with a grinding disc.

used but not many modellers have these tools.

It is unlikely that this style of clutch and flywheel fitting will allow the flywheel to run out of true but if it does, try fitting it in various different positions until the best compromise is found.

Prepare the clutch shoes in accordance with the manufacturer's recommendations. With all-metal shoes I advise some careful tweaking until the shoes fit the shape of the clutch bell exactly. (See Fig. 27).

The PTFE (white plastic) clutch shoes need cutting from a complete ring. Instructions will be given as to the correct amount to trim away, but don't trim away too much, since this will cause the clutch to engage at very high revs and make the car very difficult to drive. Remove all burrs carefully, as failure to do so will cause a very rapid rate of breakage of the "O" ring style of spring usually fitted to this type of clutch. Also de-burr the holes for the pivot pins, since stickiness here will stop the clutch from working smoothly.

Now you can turn your attention to the ball-races. These are usually single-row sealed races or an unsealed roller race. The former are more expensive but will often give a longer life than the low cost roller bearing. Both must be properly lubricated and assembled in scrupulously clean conditions. I soak ball-races in a good quality oil, not the aerosol "penetrating" type although aerosol chain lubricant is good. In many instances with ball-race clutches it is possible to insert extra bearings between the standard flanged races. Although initially this seems expensive,

the result is a well nigh "bullet-proof" clutch.

Slip the clutch bell onto the spindle and check that neither the ends of the pivot pins nor the shoes rub as the drum is spun. If either do, then cure the problem before proceeding on to the next stage.

ENGINE MOUNTING BLOCKS

If you are lucky enough to have universal engine mounts in your kit, or blocks make specifically for your engine, simply bolt the engine to the blocks. Do use a thread-locking compound here

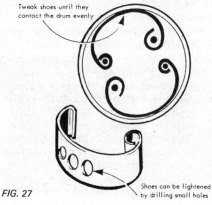

Tweak shoes until they contact the drum evenly

FIG. 27

Shoes can be lightened by drilling small holes

and bolt the blocks down into the buggy before finally tightening up the engine fixing bolts. With many engines it is a distinct help to remove the heat-sink cylinder head and use a screwdriver-handled socket wrench if Allen head bolts are used.

For the poor unfortunate that has undrilled engine blocks there are two alternatives – either drill and tap appropriate threads in the blocks or drill a hole right through the blocks and use countersunk head bolts up through from the underside. The latter is by far the easiest solution but least satisfactory from an engineering standpoint. Marking the blocks to suit your engine is done as follows:

a) Stick a piece of masking tape on to the top surface of the blocks.
b) Fit the blocks to the buggy and position the engine to obtain proper gear mesh.
c) Mark through the holes in the engine mounting lugs onto the masking tape with a sharp pencil.
d) Centre punch the position for the holes. If you don't have a centre punch, a masonry nail will do.

Now either drill and countersink or drill and tap suitable threads, use paraffin to lubricate the tap when cutting threads in aluminium.

The engine can now be fitted securely to the blocks ready for final mounting.

EXHAUST SYSTEMS

Virtually all manufacturers of buggy kits produce exhaust manifolds for the common engines. In this case other than buying the correct manifold for your engine and bolting it to the engine there is little else to do. However, if you are in the unhappy position of finding your chosen combination is not so easily fitted, you will have to take your ready mounted engine down to the model shop and look through the stock until you find something suitable. The P.B. Racing rubber tube manifold and exhaust system has much in its favour and will probably adapt well to many situations. A visit to a plumbing supplier will reveal an amazing array of different bends and elbows. Don't be tempted to use the type with soft solder already applied, as the high temperature of the engine exhaust will melt this. Don't rely on silicone tubing to carry exhaust gases; this material is only a sealer. Rely on the metal parts either fitting over one another or at least butting up to within 1mm. Secure the silicone tubing with nylon tie-wraps and always make sure that the ends of the silicone do not have any nicks or splits that could develop.

FITTING CARBURETTORS

I do not recommend fitting carburettors with epoxy glue but do recommend sealing with silicone sealer of the bath caulking type. Check before fitting the carburettor that there is no bearing lubricating passage that might be blocked with sealant. It might also be necessary to file a small clearance notch in the carburettor.

Use thread-lock on grub screws if they are used, but the cotter pin style clamp does not usually need this. Once fitted, smear a little silicone sealant over all the joint area including the ends of the clamping screws to prevent air leaks. Don't tighten screws as this can distort the mounting stub of the carburettor.

FUEL SYSTEMS

The fuel system forms an important part of the powerplant of the buggy and correct installation is important if the

Checking clutch nut and pivot pins with a square-ended rule.

engine is to run properly and reliably. The fuel tank should comply with the International standard for buggies of 125cc capacity. There is no reason why a larger tank should not be fitted for pure fun driving, but for racing the size is limited. Just in case the ingenious get the idea that the way to get round a limit on tank size is to use a very long feed pipe, the capacity includes whatever length of feed pipe the driver fits!

The "system" includes tank, feed pipe or tube, filter and pressure system if fitted. The tank needs to be sited close up to the engine and with the top of the fuel when the tank is full only just above the level of the carburettor jet. If it is any higher, the fuel will flood through to the engine while the car is standing with a full tank. The tank should be fitted with a spring-loaded top with a neck of around 10-15 mm internal diameter so that fuel can be quickly put into the tank and air can escape round the filler during filling.

With the large bore carburettors fitted to modern buggy engines some form of pressurisation of the fuel system is, if not essential, helpful to the engine at full throttle. To pressurise the fuel the exhaust pressure is used by tapping into the silencer. The expanding exhaust gases are quite a bit above atmospheric pressure, more than enough to drive the turbo-charger in many recent full-size cars, for example. A small nipple is fitted to the silencer in any convenient place (better on the upper side or else waste oil will be pumped back into the fuel tank) and connected to the fuel tank with a length of fuel tubing. This should be about 200mm long to stop fuel

syphoning back into the silencer when the throttle is closed.

The effectiveness of the silencer pressure system can best be seen when the pipe comes off! An immediate sign of this happening is that the engine appears to be running with a very weak mixture and may even stop dead.

Between tank and carburettor you should fit a filter. This should be one of the special buggy types that are transparent and quite large. Although, as explained, the size of the filter will not give the driver any tank capacity advantage it will be a great help if the car turns over. If this happens the pick-up pipe in the tank will not be able to reach the fuel and until the car is turned back onto its wheels, the only fuel that it has to run on will be that contained in the fuel feed-pipe and filter.

FINAL TOUCHES
When you finally bolt the engine into the buggy make certain that the clutch ballraces are not pre-loaded by allowing a running clearance between clutch gear and the main gear. Turn both gears through several turns, noting any tight spots and adjust until there is a clearance at the tightest spot.

Tightly meshed gears are a sure-fire route to rapid bearing wear. Last of all fit an air filter.

CHAPTER 8

Electric Speed Control

It goes without saying that some form of speed control is essential for an electric powered buggy. Almost all kits include a speed controller, usually an electro-mechanical device of some sort.

By "electro-mechanical" it is meant that the controller has moving parts as well as the electrical elements. This style of controller is frequently referred to as a "resistor controller" because the actual regulation of the drive current is effected by an electrical resistor.

For many people the electro-mechanical concept conflicts too much with the essentially electronic nature of the buggy and they therefore choose to fit electronic controllers. Some types are totally "solid state" and have no moving parts at all, but often a "turbo" relay is fitted either for reverse operation or full power or both.

RESISTOR CONTROLLERS

Most buggy builders will opt to fit the controller supplied in the kit for their first attempt at a buggy and this is almost certain to be a resistor controller. Several different types of resistor controller are available and all need a servo to operate them. Most common is the switched resistor type, which incorpo-

rates a servo driven switcher plate rotating a pair of contacts over either an etched printed circuit board or across further contacts. As the moving contact or wiper touches the fixed contacts, various fixed value resistors are switched into the circuit connecting the motor to the nicad drive batteries. Two or three steps are usually considered sufficient to give adequate speed control, although a common tune-up modification is to increase the number of steps to provide a finer degree of response to the throttle.

A smoother, proportional control can be achieved by using a large variable resistor to place an infinitely variable resistance between motor and drive battery.

Both types of controller can incorporate reverse, the former usually by means of carefully designed switcher plate tracks, the latter either by combining a switcher plate with the resistor or by fitting a reverse micro-switch to the circuit. It is also usual to provide electrical, or "dynamic", braking facilities in the set-up. Dynamic braking relies on the fact that the drive motor will act as a dynamo when spun over (i.e. when the drive current is shut off and the wheels drive the motor) and by placing an electrical load on the motor, in the form of a resistor, the motor can be very positively braked. This dynamic braking can be surprisingly powerful but is usually most noticeable at high speeds.

Generally speaking resistor controllers appeal to drivers because they feel that they are able to see how the device works and easily spot anything that has gone wrong. This is certainly true, it is easy to spot obvious faults such as broken wires and wiper arms that do not contact switcher plates, but to get good results from a resistor controller, maintenance is vital.

To start with, the controller works by resisting the flow of electricity from motor to battery and the resistance that restricts the flow actually uses electricity and converts it into heat, not into power at the wheels of the buggy. All of the wiring, plugs and sockets and the speed controller contribute to the resistance so the first important check is that all

the wiring is of sufficient size to carry the current, that plugs and sockets fitted are scrupulously clean and that solder joints are properly made. It is possible to lose up to 10 per cent of the available power through poor quality wiring on a buggy, even when the controller is supposedly in the full power position.

Next check that the moving contacts on the switcher or wiper board are clean. Use a small piece of fine emery cloth or paper to clean these contacts. Also emery cloth the fixed contacts and the contact area on the windings of the large resistor if a variable resistor controller is fitted. Now check that the pressure of the wiper is sufficient to give a good electrical contact through the whole travel of the wiper. If there is a linkage involved, it is as well to check that the various joints within this are free, as a tight spot can cause the wiper to be lifted clear of resistor or switcher plate. The common clue to poor wiper contact is pitting of the switcher contacts or circuit board. This pitting is

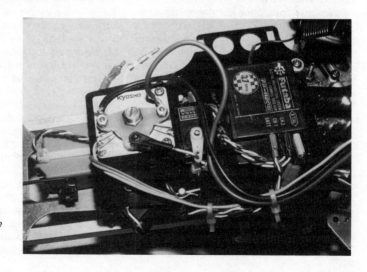

A resistor controller. The servo rotates the T-shaped switch plate to bridge pairs of contacts, connecting different resistors.

caused by sparks jumping the gap between a poorly contacting wiper and its board or contact.

Last of all examine any resistors in the circuit for signs of physical damage. This may be in the form of cracked insulation or burning of windings caused by overloading. Wire-wound resistors for variable resistor controllers are particularly susceptible to burn out. The ceramic cored, flat wire-wound types are not immune but better than the Paxolin cored, round wire variety. The fixed resistors switched into circuit by switcher plates are usually standard forms of electronic components and, as they are totally encapsulated, not readily checked for damage. Needless to say, if there is any sign of a crack in the insulation the resistor should be replaced. A badly burned appearance could also indicate imminent failure but remember that these devices work by converting electricity into heat, so some evidence of warmth is inevitable!

ON EFFICIENCY

A resistor controller is only as good as its maintenance. Don't ever believe, just because the buggy moves forwards and backwards as the R/C transmitter is operated, that the controller is working to its fullest potential. It is likely that a well-maintained resistor controller may give as good an efficiency as an electronic equivalent, but on balance the electronic system offers less scope for neglect so is probably the better bet. There is a strong argument that says because of the progressive build-up to minimum resistance and maximum voltage as a wiper slides over a resistor, finite current consumption will be less than with an electronic type that uses a relay. The latter almost instantaneously applies full voltage to the motor which,

when in electrical terms is "cold", has minimum resistance and thus draws maximum current. The more gradual build-up to full voltage, even though it is only a fraction of a second, could result in a tiny reduction in total power consumption.

ELECTRONIC CONTROLLERS

Electronic controllers are really almost the first step in tuning up a buggy. Most buggies will be a little easier to drive and response to transmitter control stick movement will almost certainly be faster. Because there are no user-serviceable parts, servicing will not be neglected and performance is probably going to be consistently better than a poorly maintained resistor controller.

It should also be remembered that if you fit an electronic controller one of the servos will be eliminated. If you are buying a new R/C system then the cost of a servo can be subtracted and the saving put towards the electronic controller.

There are disadvantages. Cost is the first hurdle to be overcome and then although, apart from water damage, physical damage is unlikely, electrical damage is all too easy to effect, so great care is needed in installation and use.

There are various types of electronic controller available and you should only pick one that is advertised as being suitable for buggy use. Although the 1/12 electric circuit racer uses the same number of cells as the buggy, the average current consumption of a buggy is very much higher and a circuit car controller will not reliably handle it. Some controllers incorporate a "Turbo Relay". This is a power by-pass switch which is designed to improve the power handling and efficiency of the controller.

Inside the controller are a number of

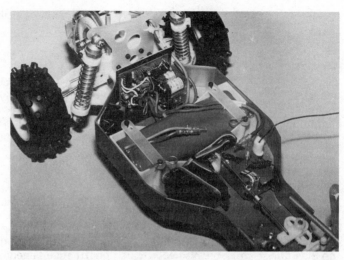

The relays on this electronic controller fitted to an Associated ¹/₁₀ buggy can be seen in their clear plastic boxes.

transistors that carry the power. These transistors use a certain amount of the variable battery power to actually "drive" them and in the final stages of the controller, the output transistor demands actually reduce the voltage available for the motor. Relays are electrically driven on/off switches that require very little current to operate, so fitting them to by-pass the output transistors saves actual current consumption and provides a higher voltage at the motor.

There are some disadvantages to relays. Firstly the contacts can become oxidised and pitted by the constant switching of high currents and they are also more easily physically damaged than transistors. If a controller has reverse and braking it will almost certainly have at least one relay, if a turbo facility is included it will have two.

NO RECEIVER BATTERY!

As well as controlling the power to the motor, the electronic controller will have a receiver battery eliminator incorporated. This means that as well as elimi-

nating one of the servos, you now also eliminate the weight of the receiver battery and its box. Most controller outputs are 6 volts, which can be a higher voltage than the dry batteries or nicads normally used. This has little effect on the receiver but will speed up the servos quite a lot. What with the reduction in weight, more rapid response to the steering as a result of the faster steering servo and the smoother faster speed control response, it is easy to see that the buggy will be transformed by fitting the electronic controller.

GOING ELECTRONIC

Once you have chosen your controller and have it in your hand, pause to read the instructions fully. Now read them again, for a mistake in wiring up can destroy the controller before the buggy turns a wheel. Transistors and other electronic components are polarity conscious, that is to say if you connect "Positive" to "Negative" you will damage something! In fact this is the most

important facet of fitting the electronic controller. Check that the leads from the battery are in fact correctly colour-coded before you start! The controller needs to be fitted into the buggy; it may be possible simply to slip the controller into the same place as the resistor controller but it is necessary to allow for a supply of cooling air over the unit, particularly if there is a heat sink on the transistors, since this needs to be kept cool. Electronics can also be very easily damaged by water, so if possible arrange for the controller to be well protected from splashes. In very wet conditions cooling air becomes of secondary importance to waterproofing – it is usually cooler when it is wet anyway.

Many controllers incorporate some means of fixing but it may be enough to simply stick the controller to the radio plate of the buggy with double sided sticky tape. Now that the controller is physically installed take look at the routing for the wires to and from it. Consider the following:

(a) Length of wires should be kept to a minimum, long wires cause a voltage drop which slows down your buggy.

(b) There should be protection for the wires, if wires flop about outside the chassis of the buggy you can guarantee that they will get caught up on something at a vital moment.

(c) It is necessary to disconnect the controller for charging the nicad battery pack.

(d) Some form of polarised connector should be fitted so that the controller can be easily connected and disconnected to switch the car on and off.

Many experienced drivers dispense with the plastic covers of polarised plugs to save weight. This is fine if you are experienced, but for beginners, don't be tempted. Keep the insulating polarised plastic cover on the plugs, the weight saving is minute.

Once all the decisions are made and you have plugs and sockets to hand you are ready to start. It is possible to do the wiring up using the mains electricity "chocolate block" style connectors but a better job by far will be made using a soldering iron. Try to adopt a logical arrangement of plugs and sockets. "Sockets" should be live, i.e. they will be fitted to battery pack and controller "Output" and "plugs" will be fitted to the motor and controller "Input". If you stick to this system you will, for example, be able to carry out simple motor tests by connecting the motor directly to the battery. A little forethought such as this makes all the difference as your quantity of equipment and level of expertise grows.

Fit the plugs and sockets as described using a soldering iron of suitable size (15 to 25 watts is ideal) and using a resin-cored electrical solder. Do watch out for "dry" joints. A good soldered joint has a smooth shiny appearance; a dull grainy appearance is wrong and should be re-soldered. Full instructions for setting up the controller will be included with the device, but do make sure that the wheels of the buggy are clear of the ground before the first experimental switch-on. In any event,

Electric racing is usually very close with frequent spills and lots of thrills.

whenever the car is switched on, the wheels will give a kick and you should be prepared for this.

Once the controller is adjusted and working, away you go. Don't stall the motor while putting full power through the controller, as this will rapidly damage it. Generally the more smoothly you drive the better you will drive and the longer your buggy will run. The most likely cause of trouble with an electronic controller is faulty connection and reverse polarity. They are well developed units that have been in use for many years and have reached a high degree of sophistication.

CHAPTER 9

Suspension and Tyres

So far, suspension has been referred to in fairly general terms with a brief explanation as to the various different types that are used for R/C buggies. A fuller explanation is necessary so that full benefit can be got from adjustment and tuning.

Suspension is a general term which refers to the whole assemblage of parts that join the wheels of the buggy to the rest. There are two reasons for fitting suspension to a full-size car, firstly to help the tyres maintain the best and most controlled contact with the running surface possible and secondly to provide as smooth a ride as possible for the passengers consistent with the primary requirement. (See Fig. 28). An R/C buggy does not need to comply with any requirements for passenger

comfort, so no compromise is needed.

As a buggy will be expected to travel over a comparatively rough surface the suspension needs to be compliant enough for the four wheels to stay in contact with ground for as much of the time as possible. This is necessary so that maximum cornering, drive and braking forces can be generated. The wheels are mounted on pivoted arms which allow them to move up and down independently to follow surface undulations. Even an R/C buggy benefits from moving on a reasonably even keel, so the theory is that the low inertia of the unsprung parts of the suspension, the wishbones, wheel hubs and wheels, allows them to move up and down rapidly whilst the greater inertia of the main bulk of the buggy causes it to stay

FIG. 28

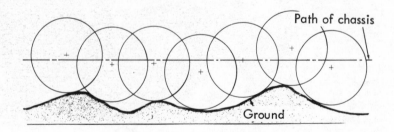

steady. Springs are fitted to help the suspension follow the surface.

A spring is an energy storage device and uncontrolled it will cause the buggy to leap wildly around. Control can be in the form of either friction damping as a result of stiff pivots and joints or more sophisticated hydraulic (oil-filled) dampers. Dampers absorb the energy that the suspension movement tries to store in the springing and dissipates it in the form of heat. The conversion of this energy to heat is done by forcing oil through tiny passages in the dampers. If damping is really well carried out the suspension will have a surprisingly dead feel to it. When the buggy is dropped sharply down on to a hard surface the suspension will compress and the springs will store the energy generated as the weight of the buggy compresses them. As this happens, the dampers compress, absorbing some of the energy warming their oil and as full suspension compression is reached, the movement reverses as the stored energy in the springs starts to push the suspension down again. There won't be

quite as much vigour there now; the dampers are doing their thing and continue to do so as the suspension moves towards its at-rest position. By the time the suspension reaches this position there will only be just about enough energy left to push the buggy up to its normal ride height and nothing left over for a bounce; bouncing back up is a sure sign that there is insufficient damping.

As well as the function of absorbing the worst of the effects of bumps, the suspension has to cope with effects that the buggy's rolling and pitching have on the steering. It is inevitable that there will be some rolling as the buggy turns corners. If the centre of gravity is above the ground, which it obviously must be, then when the buggy corners, a rolling force is inevitable. If the buggy rolls the wheels should not roll with it and the suspension links are designed to keep the wheels and thus the tyres at the optimum angle for traction. Similarly with fore and aft pitching, which can affect the steering badly, so suspension design must be modified to cope.

Coil spring suspension with dampers inside the coils are used with double wishbones on this rear end assembly.

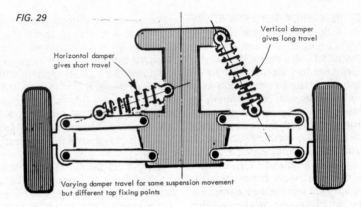

FIG. 29

Horizontal damper
gives short travel

Vertical damper
gives long travel

Varying damper travel for same suspension movement
but different top fixing points

SPRINGS

As described above, springs are fitted to help the wheels follow the surface undulations. Springs can be of various types, torsion bars, leaf springs, hairpin springs or coil springs. Each has its own peculiar strengths and weaknesses. By far the most commonly used is the coil spring, usually in a mode that causes the spring to be compressed under load. This can be either by direct coupling to the wishbone or suspension link or via a cantilever. Many buggies include provision for spring adjustment and it is important to remember that this adjustment only affects the ride height of the car. In practice increasing

the ride height may have two effects. Firstly it can appear to make the suspension "softer" in action, as the buggy will not bottom out on the ground so frequently. Conversely, body roll will be more pronounced because the buggy is higher. So one can easily see that simply altering spring compression preload is a double-edged sword, and one that should be applied with caution.

Really altering the character of the suspension springing very much requires a change of spring or a change in the mounting points. This latter course can dramatically change the character of the spring, as moving the attachment point will vary the rate of spring compression compared with suspension movement and is a far more powerful tuning aid than almost any other. By fixing the spring at different points it is possible to choose any compromise between a setting that compresses the spring rapidly during the first part of the suspension travel and slowly thereafter or slowly to begin with then speeding up, two totally different characters with the same spring and same ride height. (See Fig. 29).

Hairpin springs are simple but effective.

A pair of dampers showing the extremes of travel.

Changing spring strength is not terribly easy for the buggy owner. It is possible to purchase alternative springs for some buggies but with others the only chance is to wind your own. Even this is not at all easy, for as well as it being difficult to achieve consistent results from the point of view of dimensions, it can be difficult to be sure that supplies of piano wire from which to make the springs will be consistent. For real ease of chopping and changing springs, torsion bars take a lot of beating. A move up or down in gauge or a slight variation in length will vary the characteristics noticeably. A tip worth remembering when making springs is to start off with equal lengths of wire and when the springs are finished, trim off the same amount of wire from each spring irrespective of the exact number of turns. If you then tweak them all to the same length, they will be fairly uniform in strength. (See Fig. 30).

DAMPERS
It has already been shown that some form of control or damping of springs is necessary. The most basic form of damping is stiff suspension joints, but the biggest failing of such an approach is inconsistency. There will be a tendency for joints gradually to free off as the buggy is driven, with a consequent continual change in suspension character. By far the best system is an oil-filled damper. Most buggy manufacturers now offer such units, either as standard

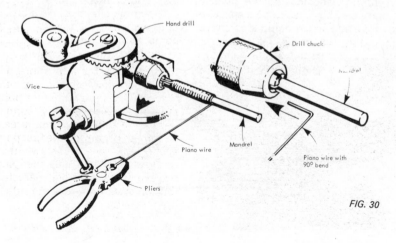

Hand drill

Drill chuck

Mandrel

Vice

Piano wire

Mandrel

Piano wire with 90° bend

Pliers

FIG. 30

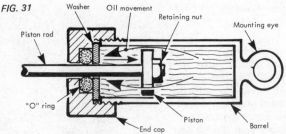

FIG. 31

Washer   Oil movement

Retaining nut

Mounting eye

Piston rod

"O" ring

End cap

Piston

Barrel

fitments on their buggies or as optional extras. Dampers have to be robustly made to stand up to the punishment, particularly as they are fairly exposed to damage. As well as being strong they need to be very well made in terms of quality of finish, as the high fluid pressure inside them will rapidly force out the oil if there are any poorly fitting joints. These provisos tend to make dampers expensive and if consistent volume or other more complex type are required, the cost goes up even more.

At their simplest, dampers are closed cylinders with a piston moving up and down inside displacing oil from one side to the other. This has the inherent problem that the piston rod is continually entering and leaving the body of the damper. There has to be a space for it to move into so the damper can never be properly full of oil. Of course, as soon as it moves out of the damper a space is left and after only a very few

cycles of operation the air in the damper bubbles up with the oil, producing an elastic froth that is not terribly efficient as a damping medium. (See Fig. 31).

Developments in damper design led to constant volume dampers that allowed for the piston rod displacement either by use of a second floating piston or by arranging for the piston rod to go right through the damper cylinder so that there is always a full length of piston rod inside. (See Fig. 32). Even the best of sealing systems can leak a little so the final refinement is an oil reservoir connected up to the damper body that allows for minute volume changes and prevents pressure build up from driving oil from the unit while enabling small losses to be made up.

Assembling dampers is a task that all buggy drivers will need to undertake at some time or another. Even if ready assembled units are supplied with a kit, they will need to be serviced. First

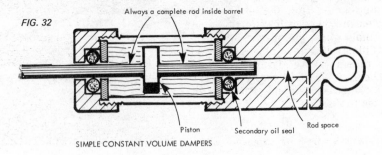

Always a complete rod inside barrel

FIG. 32

Piston   Secondary oil seal   Rod space

SIMPLE CONSTANT VOLUME DAMPERS

76

Reservoirs for damper fluid are sometimes fitted.

requirement is absolute cleanliness. Rebuilding dampers is not a task that should be attempted beside a race track. It will be cheaper in the long run to purchase a spare set of dampers than to start to dismantle them on the trackside. Only a tiny scratch on a neoprene oil-seal will ruin it and only a few specks of grit inside the damper will see it soon grind itself to bits. Many instruction books recommend sealing the ends of dampers with silicone sealant, but I have found this next to impossible, as the oil turns the silicone to liquid and washes it off the joint long before a proper seal has been made. Instead use PTFE plumbers' and gas-fitters' jointing tape, which really does seal up the threads but allows the joints to be easily dismantled.

Often the manufacturing process can mark the spindles or piston rods of dampers, so it is a good idea to polish them with oiled wet or dry emery paper before assembly. It goes without saying that all traces of abrasive must be washed off before any more work is done on the damper. If you are about to service a damper thoroughly, clean the outside before attempting to take it to pieces. Once it is in bits clean all the parts straight away before wrapping them up in a clean tissue. Examine spindles and oil seals for signs of wear and obtain replacement parts if necessary. Either drill a piece of wood to hold the dampers up on end or use a blob of Plasticene; it will be necessary to leave them for a few minutes for any air bubbles to disperse.

An assembled damper and its component parts.

Wind a layer of PTFE tape on to the screw-in end piece and lightly oil the seals. Slide the piston and rod assembly into the cylinder slowly to allow the oil to flow round the piston. With all dampers it will be necessary to seal them up progressively unless they are fitted with an overflow reservoir or bleed screw. Tighten the end-cap a little and push in the piston. If it won't go all the way to the end of its travel, loosen the end cap and push down the piston which will allow a little oil to escape. Try again with the end cap screwed down

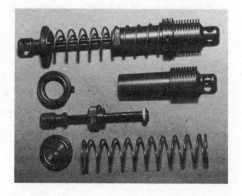

and repeat the bleeding operation as many times as is necessary until the piston moves to the full extent of its travel.

Part of the damping characteristic of the damper will be related to its detail design but a large part will be down to the type of fluid used. Most dampers are designed to be filled with one of the many grades of lubricating oil available. Some may be filled with hydraulic fluid. Do not use the wrong type of fluid in any damper, it may well attack the seals. The oil in the damper is intended to get warm as the suspension moves up and down and all oils change their viscosity as temperature changes. As the oil heats up it will thin down and the damper will change in character. Too much heat and the oil may well start to vaporise, causing a complete breakdown in the proper operation of the damper. Larger dampers are a help here because, firstly, there is more oil and, secondly, there is more metal in the damper to radiate heat. Some manufacturers supply finned sleeves to slide over dampers.

In general the grade of oil should be chosen so that the damper has dissipated all the energy that it is required to just as the buggy rebounds to its correct static position. If the oil is too thick it will not return to the correct position, if it is too thin it will bounce as the suspension moves through more than the single cycle required of it. If the oil is dramatically over-viscous then instead of the suspension smoothly compressing and being finely controlled by the damper as the buggy hits its first bump, the spring will not be able to compress properly and the buggy will be thrown into the air.

Usually, the very last thing to do to control bounce is to put thicker oil in the dampers. If in spite of filling dampers with the thinnest grade of oil obtainable, it still seems that there is too much damping, then the only thing left to do is to arrange for the oil to move from one side of the damper piston to the other more easily. This can be done either by increasing the size of the holes in the piston or by filing a flat on the side of the piston. Proceed with caution, although if you do take off too much the situation can be recouped by filling the damper with thicker oil!

TOE-IN, TOE-OUT

Most buggies benefit from having the front wheels pointing inwards a little. If the buggy seems unstable on the straight then try a little more toe-in but don't go too far, otherwise the drag resulting will slow down the buggy and also very rapidly scrub out the tyres. If the buggy persists in weaving on the straight take a look at the steering linkages for stiffness and consider whether your choice of tyres is correct. On the latest generation of four-wheel steering buggies there is a whole new world of experiment available with toe-in and toe-out, for these are now adjustable at both ends. By and large this adjustment should be thought of as taking up the inevitable tiny amounts of free movement in the suspension joints, and in the case of four-wheel drive buggies this can be multiplied as the power is applied to the buggy. Proceed with caution, only making one small adjustment at a time and noting the effect, preferably in writing, before trying another adjustment. The foregoing should apply to any and all suspension adjustments: proceed in a methodical fashion and you may just end up with a better setting than the manufacturer advised in the first place.

Tyre types. L. to r. General purpose spiked front and rear, centre lug mud tyre, standard mud front and rear, straight ribbed front.

Summing up, the ideal suspension is one which allows the buggy to lollop along without hitting the ground, only rolling a moderate amount on corners so that steering is unaffected, with wheels that accurately follow every undulation without any sign of bounce causing the wheels to break contact with the ground. To achieve this there should be long suspension travels with generous ground clearance – large wheels are an advantage here, together with soft springs and progressive damping. Most kit cars go a long way towards achieving these ideals but there is always room for a dedicated owner to come along and improve things.

TYRE CHOICE

As the topic of tyre choice is a major variable even on the same day on the same track, this has been left until last. Within reason once the suspension is tuned to suit the driver's style and the power available, beyond altering the actual ride height a little to take into account the particular surface being raced on, the single biggest factor affec-

ting handling will be the choice of tyre. Depending on the balance of grip between front and rear and overall, the buggy can change from a docile easy-to-drive charmer to a viciously uncontrollable beast as quickly as you change the tread pattern.

There are several different tyre tread types around, Block Tread (similar to normal road tyres), Spiked Tyres (great for grass) and Mud tyres – obvious what they are for! Broadly speaking all can be used on any surface but they will all give a differing amount of grip. It is unwise to be too narrow-minded where buggy tyres are concerned; although a tyre may be sold as a "Mud Tyre" it may be that on any particular surface it is just the right tyre for the degree of moisture and looseness of surface prevailing. Be broad-minded and try anything you have available until you find the right combination.

In general terms, if your buggy understeers, i.e. tries to go straight on at corners, there are two approaches: (a) more grip from the front tyres, or (b) less grip from the rear tyres. If, however, it turns in too tightly then you must reduce the grip from the front tyres or increase the grip from the rear. Do be honest with yourself over this aspect, are you perhaps trying to go too fast round the corner anyway?

As well as differing tread patterns it is possible to get tyres of differing width. Try making up a set of wheels with front tyres on rear hubs and, in the case of narrow rear tyres, put a set of these on front hubs. It is almost always beneficial to puncture the tyres, for as they are part of the unsprung weight of the car they will provide their own suspension. A solid tyre is not a good idea, since however well the rest of the suspension works the tyre will have a mind of its own. Some drivers go as far as to cut discs out of the tyre walls to lighten them and thus reduce unsprung weight. The size of the hole is not seemingly important, providing it allows the tyre to deform fairly easily, and it is usually better to drill a hole in the wheel hub rather than the tyre as a hole in the tyre may start a tear.

CHAPTER 10

Engine Operation

Difficulties in starting and adjusting the engine have probably put more people off I.C. buggies than any other factor. Straight away it should be said that too many kits for buggies and most engine manufacturers give no indication at all as to how these problems should be approached or any clues as to the pitfalls.

In a previous chapter the operating principles of the engines were described but no attempt was made to explain how the engines were actually started.

You will firstly need to gather a number of pieces of equipment together. It is possible to improvise on some of them but to my mind this simply puts off the evil hour when money has to be spent and only makes the task more difficult. The requirements are as follows:

(a) Fuel. A supply of fuel containing 10% nitro-methane (nitro) and preferably synthetic oil.

(b) A fuelling bulb. To transfer fuel from the bulk supply to the buggy tank.

(c) Two volt battery. For heating the glow plug (plug) element. The best type is the self-contained variety with built in meter to indicate both battery and plug condition.

(d) A glow-plug. Not always supplied with the engine.

(e) A glow clip. To connect up the plug to the battery.

(f) Starter. A 12 volt Hi-Torque type fitted with a rubber drive ring, or start cone for some types of buggy.

(g) Twelve volt battery. To power the starter.

(h) Your R/C transmitter. You will need to be able to operate the throttle.

If expense is no object, it is possible to purchase a total starter box unit which simply requires hooking up to a 12 volt battery and then provides the glow plug power source and turns over the engine. Such boxes can be adjusted to fit most buggies. You should also have handy suitable size screwdrivers or spanners to make any necessary adjustments to the carburettor. It sounds and is quite a list of bits and pieces but all are needed and must be taken into account when the purchase is first costed out. Remember, once the engine starts up it will make quite a fair bit of noise and if you have sensitive neighbours wait until they are out and don't start to try the engine out late at night!

First things first. Hook up the starter

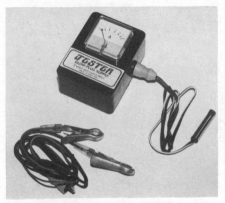

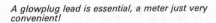

A glowplug lead is essential, a meter just very convenient!

and experiment to find out which way round you have got to hook it up to the 12 volt battery. The buggy engine must rotate anti-clockwise when viewed from the crankshaft end (See Fig. 34). Connect up the glow clip to the 2 volt battery and

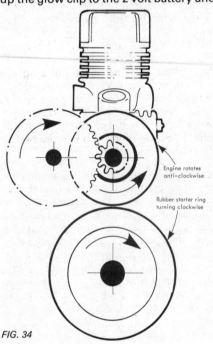

Engine rotates anti-clockwise

Rubber starter ring turning clockwise

FIG. 34

check out the plug. Make a mental note of the meter reading with a freshly charged glow battery, which will be a big help later on, as if the battery starts to go flat you will be able to see straight away. It is a good idea to fix the rubber ring onto the starter with cyano glue before proceeding. Don't spin the starter until the cyano is absolutely cured, otherwise it may spray into your face with very unpleasant consequences. Before fuelling up try a few experimental bursts with the starter to find out the easiest way of holding buggy and starter. When you feel happy about your basic technique then you can fuel up and really get down to it!

Switch on your transmitter and receiver and check out the throttle operation. With the tank full, open the main fuel needle valve 2½ to 3 turns and spin the engine over with the starter until you see the fuel run up the tubing to the carburettor. This is helped if the buggy is kept more or less level, but in the case of trouble, put your finger over the exhaust and as the engine spins, exhaust pressure will force the fuel up the line. Once the fuel has reached the engine, connect up the glow plug and re-apply the starter. Providing that the plug is glowing properly and there is fuel present in the engine in the correct proportions with air, then the engine should start. If you have followed the foregoing instructions, then it certainly should! As most engine manufacturers set up carburettors roughly at the factory, the setting should be close enough for the engine to run in some way. Try to keep the engine going with very

Serpent Cobra *sitting on top of a starter box which contains glowplug energiser and starter.*

gentle "blips" of the throttle, but don't open it wide – only tiny amounts to start with. If it seems happy to keep running disconnect the glow plug and leave it alone for a few moments to warm up.

IT WON'T START

Although it doesn't happen too often, there is the possibility that nothing will happen when you try to start up. Four possibilities exist:

(a) No compression – very unlikely with a new engine, but do check that the plug is tightened. Far more likely to be the opposite, too much compression. If you cannot turn the engine over, try loosening the glow plug two or three turns while you start up. Once the engine is running you can tighten it up and the technique will gradually become redundant as the engine is run-in.

(b) No fuel – a possibility. Check that you have opened the needle valve three turns from the point where it shuts off the fuel, not from the point where it is screwed up hard against the end of the threads, not always one and the same thing. It may be necessary actually to unscrew the needle three or four or more turns to "open" it 2 to 3 turns!

(c) Too much fuel – you may have

overdone the exhaust pressure priming, and this is usually indicated by raw fuel spraying from the exhaust outlet. Close the needle valve and spin the engine over with the plug removed – place a cloth over the top of the engine first to avoid spraying fuel everywhere. Start again.

(d) No glow – this should be easily noticed if you have a meter in the circuit but if you have not, take the plug out and connect it up to the battery and take a look. There should be a bright orange glow; a dull red is not good enough. After you have taken the plug out to check several times you will appreciate the value of a meter.

KEEPING IT GOING

By the time you have disconnected the glow-plug and moved the starting gear to one side the chances are that the engine has stopped. It may be that it would not keep running at all without continual blipping of the throttle. If this is the case adjust the throttle stop screw to speed up the tick-over. (See Fig. 35) If the tick-over is too fast, slow it down! Maybe the engine just refuses to keep running for long at all. If this is the case, try to observe how it actually stops. If it appears to choke up with a large amount of smoke and quantities of raw fuel coming out of the exhaust, then it is too rich and you should close down the main needle valve half a turn and try again. If on the other hand the motor revs briefly and stops abruptly then it needs more fuel. Open the main needle valve.

The aim must be to achieve some sort of setting of the main needle valve that will keep the engine running. When this is achieved (and don't expect it to tick over too well — you will probably have to continue to blip the throttle to keep it going) then you can adjust the full throttle needle valve setting. This must be done before any attempt is made to set the idle mixture.

Be careful here, although the method described works well. If carried out carelessly it can result in melted drive gears and clutch shoes. Hold the buggy

down on the ground so that the wheels cannot turn and briefly open the throttle fully. The needle valve should be adjusted so that the motor runs flat out and cleanly with the clutch slipping. This generates a lot of heat in the clutch, this is why it should only be done for short periods with time allowed in between runs for things to cool down. By setting the needle valve in this way you will fairly closely duplicate the fuel requirements of the motor when it is running flat out on the track.

With main needle setting approximately correct, the idle mixture can be set up. Blip the throttle and observe the engine's reaction. If it coughs and splutters and gives out clouds of smoke before picking up to a clean full throttle run, the idle mixture is too rich. Close down the mixture control screw half a turn and try again. On the other hand, a weak or lean setting is shown by the engine immediately dying as the throttle is quickly opened. Once the mixture is correct, the engine should tick-over on the trackside for as long as you wish it to and then pick up cleanly on demand.

FIRST PRINCIPLES

It is possible that the carburettor setting is so far away from the correct point that the motor will not function at all. This can be as a result of an overhaul or continual abortive attempts to adjust it. To arrive at a basic setting you will need to remove the air filter so that you can look down the barrel. Find a spare piece of clean fuel tubing and then drain the fuel from your buggy. Start by closing down the main needle valve completely and re-opening it 2½ to 3 turns. Now look down the carburettor and adjust the tick-over screw (throttle-stop screw) until the throttle barrel is open between ½ and 1 mm. Now close down the idle

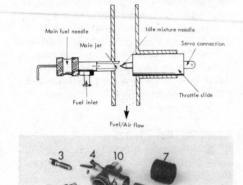

FIG. 35 1. Main needle valve. 2. Fuel inlet nipple. 3. Adjustable idle jet. 4. Slow running adjustment screw. 5. Throttle slide. 6. Carburettor body. 7. Dust protection bellows. 8. Idle needle. 9. Servo connection. 10. Mounting stub.

mixture adjustment screw until it completely shuts off the fuel to the carburettor. You can identify this point by connecting up the fuel tubing to the nipple on the carburettor and gently blowing down it as you close the needle, Now, with the throttle barrel or slide against the stop, blow gently down the fuel tubing and slowly open the idle mixture adjustment screw until you can blow air slightly through the jet. This will indicate the setting that will just allow fuel to enter the carburettor even with the throttle closed.

On many carburettors that have adjustable needles rather than jets, PB Slide for example, a good guide to a starting point is to set the needle to just exit from the jet with the throttle slide half-way open. The blow test can be used with all types of carburettor with automatic mixture control, whether they are slide or barrel types.

ON THE TRACK
Setting up the engine in the pits is only half the story, the object of that exercise being simply to get the engine running well enough to drive the buggy without it continually stopping. Once out on the track try a few gentle laps without over-revving the engine. If the engine is brand new, it is a good idea to run a full tank of fuel through it at modest speed and gradually build up to full throttle on the straights as you run through subsequent tanks. Try bursts of full throttle on short straights first and take note of what happens as you open the throttle.

The response will indicate whether the mixture strengths are correct in just the same way on the track as they did when the buggy was in the pits. Too lean and the engine will die, too rich and it will smoke heavily before speeding up and may die. If the buggy shows any sign of "running out of breath" on the straights, return to the pits immediately and open up the main needle a little. If you run the motor flat out on the straight with too little fuel going through it then a seizure is sure to follow and that can mean a ruined engine. Try to run the engine always a little richer than the optimum, as this way you may lose a few hundreds of RPM but you will keep an engine!

Although synthetic oils are generally very good from the point of view of lubrication when the engine is properly set up, in adverse conditions they neither indicate maladjustment as well as castor based fuels nor protect as well. For this reason many drivers use a few per cent (3 or 4) of castor oil in their fuel. This has the advantage of showing more smoke than synthetic oil fuel and gives a visual check on mixture setting. No smoke, too lean, too much smoke, too rich.

Slide carburettor as supplied with many engines.

Using a starter in rim friction contact with the engine flywheel; starter must rotate in opposite direction to engine.

AIR AND FUEL FILTERS

Both fuel and air should be properly filtered before it reaches the engine. Failure to filter will wreck the engine very very quickly – as little as 10 minutes' running on a dusty track can be enough to wear out a piston and cylinder. Wear does not stop at piston and cylinder, as the crankshaft and bearings are likely to be ruined as well.

Fan-folded paper air filters are best and ideally should be coupled up to a first stage filter of oil-impregnated plastic foam. It is not good enough simply to push the filter over the top of the carburettor, it must be properly sealed with a silicone sealant. The bath caulking sealants are ideal, such nice colours too! Do check to make sure the actual element is properly sealed into the filter body also. A fuel filter is not so much a protection for the engine as a guard against frustration. The engine is likely to stop with a blockage before the sort of dirt that can get through the tiny passages in the carburettor does much harm. Fit one anyway, for however

carefully you might filter fuel into your filler, there will always be some that gets into the tank.

TUNE-UP TIPS

Once the buggy is actually up and running, you will probably find that it takes quite a few weeks of practice at driving before you are really able to take full advantage of the power that is available. Once you have got used to it, you may well decide that you would like it to go faster, have better acceleration, and generally have a little more sparkle.

GEAR RATIOS

The first area to take a look at in the chase after performance is the gear ratio. This is the ratio of the number of turns the engine makes to one turn of the driven wheels. Each different engine develops its peak power at different revolutions per minute (RPM) and should ideally demand a different gear ratio. A slow-revving engine may have enough power to drive the buggy just as fast as its high-revving counterpart,

Direct friction to flywheel or crankshaft with starter pad or cone requires starter to turn in same direction as engine.

but if the same ratio is fitted then it will be revving at full speed and the buggy will be moving comparatively slowly.

When talking of gear ratios, the term "high" ratio means a small reduction between engine and wheels: the engine turns slowly yet the buggy moves quickly. A "low" ratio is the opposite, the engine turns at high speed, the buggy travels slowly. As well as matching the ratio to the particular engine, it must also be matched to the track for best performance. If you notice that someone else's buggy seems to have much more "get up and go" than your own it is most probable that the gear ratio is the major difference.

For tracks with short straights and tight corners a "low" ratio is needed so that the engine can speed up to full RPM and thus full power. If you try to use the same "low" ratio on a track with a long straight then you will be asking for trouble, for the engine will reach peak RPM long before it reaches the end of the straight and may well carry on to increase in RPM well above the

safe limit and literally blow up inside. The engine should reach a peak about three-quarters of the way down the longest straight and only sustain peak RPM for a very few seconds.

If you do fit a lower ratio than you have been used to, you will find the buggy quite a bit more difficult to drive as there will seem to be a lot more power available at the rear wheels. At first this will make the car much easier to spin and will cause it to understeer more out of corners. You must become more skilled at applying the power available, only throwing the throttle wide open sharply when the buggy is pointing straight ahead. In adverse conditions a low ratio is a distinct liability; always go to a higher than optimum ratio for engine and track if the surface is wet, when your car will be much easier to drive and you will be able to concentrate on driving smoothly instead of fighting the buggy.

CLUTCH SLIP
Coupled with gear ratios in the search

for improved driveability and "snap" is the amount of slip present in the clutch. The buggy clutch can be thought of as a crude form of automatic transmission or torque converter. As the engine throttle is opened centrifugal force starts to cause the clutch shoes to fly outwards to contact the inside of the clutch drum. It will be realised that if the shoes are heavy then they will fly out at low RPM and vice-versa. If the engine develops its maximum power at very high RPM then with heavy clutch shoes the clutch will be fully engaged before the engine is developing anything like its full power. This produces a buggy that is sluggish away from the start line and lacking in response when the throttle is opened. The reverse is the clutch that is too light that engages with a bang at high power and full throttle which causes the buggy to spin easily and may not give full drive at any time.

A compromise has to be reached that will produce a clutch that engages as the RPM reach a point where the engine is producing reasonable power but doesn't come in with a bang at high RPM. Start off with the clutch set as instructed and before starting to experiment with different weight shoes do make sure that you have a spare set of standard shoes to go back to if your experiments take too much off the shoes. A slipping clutch is definitely to be avoided. If the clutch is slipping heat will be generated and in extreme cases may cause plastic drive gears to fail and also ruin bearings in the clutch.

MORE NITRO?

The simplest way of upping the power of your buggy is to use more nitro in the fuel. Do make sure that you are making the best of the power available before looking for more, though. Certainly using more nitro in the fuel is a quick and easy way to getting more power, but it is expensive.

However, almost any increase in power will be at a price, maybe in terms of cost of bolt-on accessories or in the hidden expense of greater fuel costs. To get more power out of the engine it is necessary to get it to burn more fuel or make better use of the fuel it is already burning. I would strongly advise against anyone trying to modify or "tune-up" their engines. The simple way is to fit a larger bore carburettor or a tuned exhaust system. The standard bore for buggy engine carburettors is 7mm and 9 or 10mm alternatives are available. It is usually possible to obtain a carburettor that is made by the engine manufacturer or a specialist replacement.

Tuned exhaust systems are a form of supercharging, working by using a carefully designed silencer that reflects the exhaust gases back towards the engine exhaust port and using these gases to compress the fuel-air mixture in the cylinder and thus get more into it. As the mixture is being transferred from crankcase to combustion chamber, both exhaust port and transfer are open at the same time so that the incoming gases can drive out the burnt gases. This usually means that there will be some fresh mixture that is able to go straight through the cylinder and in the absence of the tuned exhaust would just escape into the atmosphere. The length of the tuned exhaust is critical: if the pipe is too short, the exhaust will be reflected back up the pipe too soon, before the mixture has started to flow out of the exhaust and into the pipe. What then happens is that instead of fresh mixture being reflected back into the cylinder, polluted exhaust gases are compressed back into the cylinder and there is no gain in power.

On the other hand, if the tuned pipe is too long, the exhaust port will be closed by the time the reflected gases get back to it and they will not be able to get in! It is most important to take note of the tuned pipe supplier's instructions when it comes to length. No two pipes will be the same and each must be set to the correct length, otherwise the results may well be a decrease in performance rather than a gain.

MAINTENANCE

Most drivers tend to clean their buggy when they return from a race meeting, but not many take the trouble to maintain the engine. Cleaning the exterior comes first. Do block up all the openings before starting, otherwise you will wash dirt into the motor instead of cleaning it.

Once the outside is clean, take out the glow-plug, remove the air-filter and spin the engine over whilst squirting "Lay-up" oil into the carburettor. If you don't have specially formulated lay-up oil, a good quality lubricating oil will do. Now with the plug back in place turn the engine over and feel the compression, which should be really positive and be retained for 30 seconds or so with the engine at top dead centre. Without

good compression the engine will not start easily, nor will it tick-over properly.

You will probably be able to feel at the same time any sign of the connecting rod big end wearing. After every other meeting is it sound common sense to take the back-plate off the engine to check visually on the condition of the big-end. Any cause for doubt is a reason to fit a new rod, as a rod breakage can mean the total end of the engine. Breakage can strain the crank, score the liner and even damage the crank-case. It isn't worth using an engine with a worn connecting rod. Take a look at the glow-plug, and if it looks at all dull, replace it. It will only work properly if it is bright and shiny.

Far and away the most common cause of engine damage will not be encountered on the track. More engines are damaged by over-revving in the pits than are on the track. Assuming that the gear ratio is something like correct it is unlikely that the engine can attain terminal RPM but with the wheels off the ground it is all too easy. The damage may not be immediately apparent but when the engine explodes half-way down the long straight remember how it screamed in anguish as you were setting up the carburettor in the pits and vow that that was the last time!

CHAPTER 11

On the Track

As the last few touches to the buggy are made thoughts will be turning to the actual driving of it. One of the delights of buggies is the possibility of being able to run them on relatively unprepared ground anywhere. It is not essential to have a purpose built track to enjoy your buggy – it can be run in your own back garden. There are a few things to remember before you rush out and drive just anywhere, though.

Electric buggy drivers have probably got more freedom than I.C. buggy drivers. Engine noise can be a real problem, although the I.C. driver is able to use ground that would be too rough for electric buggies. There are advantages and disadvantages to both types of buggy. Therefore, in the first instance choose a piece of ground that is not too rough for your buggy and if it is an I.C. buggy, make sure you are not going to annoy anyone with the noise. Wherever you choose to run your buggy, whether it is an I.C. or electric-type, you should be very aware of the effect of running your model. It will probably attract people, especially young children, who

Dust is a major problem with I.C. cars; a good air filter is essential.

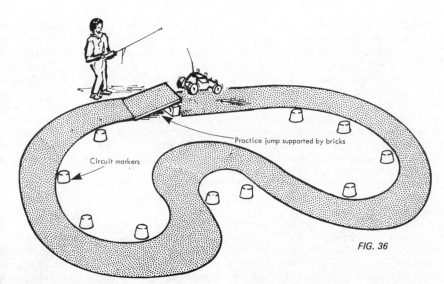

Circuit markers

Practice jump supported by bricks

FIG. 36

may rush over to watch and it may well attract domestic animals, particularly dogs, which seem to be particularly attracted to chasing buggies!

There is nothing wrong in principle in having an audience, but remember that you are a total beginner to driving a buggy and that if something does go very wrong and you hit a spectator or someone's property, you could be held liable. Running a buggy in a public place does demand some degree of responsibility towards the public and everyone who runs a buggy in a public place should be insured. Even if you have taken out suitable insurance, you will need to take some action to keep bystanders out of the way of your buggy. Above all, don't show off. About the only thing you are likely to demonstrate is your own ineptitude until you have had quite a lot of driving practice!

IMPROVE YOUR SKILL

Anyone can drive a buggy at high speed around a wide-open patch of ground.

To actually improve your skill at controlling your buggy you will need to set out some sort of training course. A few plastic or even paper plates can be laid out in a simple pattern around the grass and you should then practise driving around them in a set pattern. Place at least two pairs of plates a couple of metres apart some distance away and work up to driving through narrow gaps a long way away at speed. It is surprisingly difficult to drive with precision when standing on the ground at more than about 30 metres away. It is even more difficult to drive through narrow gaps while the buggy is going round corners.

If your buggy has reverse, and even I.C. buggies have reverse now, you will need continually to use it, performing three point turns and reversing the car round twisty parts of the circuit. Reverse will not be much use to you in racing if when you need to use it you turn the wrong way because of too little practice beforehand.

91

TRACK DISCIPLINE

At some time sooner or later you are almost sure to want to try your hand at driving your buggy round a proper circuit. You do not have to go to race meetings to do this, although unless you join a club, racing is probably your only chance. Even joining a club doesn't mean that you have to compete with your buggy. There are many people who just drive their buggies for fun, in fact more drive for fun than ever race them.

Before you turn up at a club track there are a number of points that you should be aware of that will help to make you a welcome visitor. To create the right impression do make sure that you turn up for your first visit properly equipped. Have a charger, 12 volt battery and so on, fresh batteries in your buggy and transmitter and if at all possible alternative frequency crystals for your R/C equipment. On arriving find a club committee member and find out what the arrangements are for getting a turn on the track. There will probably be some sort of frequency control in operation and it is vital that you fully understand the system in use before setting up your gear. Once you have unpacked your gear and charged up your buggy it is probably a good idea to go and walk round the track and watch any buggies that are running before you have a go. If there are several people waiting to use the frequency you are on why not offer to act as a marshall for a while?

Marshalls are an essential part of buggy running or racing on any sort of permanent track, particularly if there is an elevated drivers' stand or "rostrum" that takes a little time to get down from. It is inevitable that from time to time buggies will either turn over or get stuck on or behind obstructions. Without a marshall, drivers would be continuously chasing across the track to rescue their own buggies. Stand in a position that won't obscure the drivers' view of the track and put cars back on the track as they become displaced. If the occasional shout of "Marshall" annoys you, let this feeling remind you not to shout yourself in similar circumstances when you take to the track a little later.

ON THE TRACK

At last it is your turn to drive. Whatever you do, don't ever believe that you will be the fastest driver at the track on your first outing, or even your second or third. Many very good international standard drivers have been shown a thing or two by club drivers on their own tracks, but those club drivers have probably used the track week after week for years.

If you can drive round for a full lap without hitting something at the first attempt you will be making a good start. The discipline of driving round a circuit is something that has to be experienced to be understood. All the practice that you have done will be a great help, though. Above all try to keep out of faster drivers' paths; move over to the side of the track on the straights and take corners wide. The hardest part of driving a buggy is to keep a watch on the others while you are going round the track at high speed and this takes hours, even months, of practice.

Once you have mastered the business of just getting round the track you will wish to try and drive a little faster. Experiment to see how fast your buggy goes down the straight, shutting off well before the corners and trying the feel of the brakes at speed. Start to

Moving from one type of surface to another is the trickiest skill to acquire of all.

position the car on the track, both to take the fastest line round corners and to avoid the worst of the bumps. With a buggy, the fastest line round a corner is often the one with the least bumps, not the line that a top Formula One Grand Prix driver would take.

If you are driving an electric buggy all of the above will have taken several charges of the batteries but could be accomplished with one tank of fuel with an I.C. buggy. Do make sure that you are not being too greedy and taking more than your fair share of track time. A maximum of 10 minutes at any one time is fair if there is more than just a single driver on the frequency.

SETTING-UP
Setting-up is the term generally applied to the process of adjusting the buggy to suit both the driver and the track to best effect. For early excursions it is definitely best simply to keep the buggy near to the standard set-up specified in the instructions. The standard set-up will have been devised by the manufacturers as a compromise that will give acceptable results in average conditions with average drivers. Until you are able to drive quite well you will not have the

ability to tell whether any alteration that you make to the buggy improves or damages its performance. Whatever you do, don't make any alteration to your buggy that is in any way permanent unless you are prepared to accept that it was a waste of time and buy parts to put it back to the original specification.

Until you are very confident of your ability to predict the results of modifications it is not a good idea to try anything other than those adjustments provided for by the manufacturer. These fall into the areas of gear ratio changes, ride height adjustment, damper rate (by changing oils) steering throw, toe-in and toe-out, alternative damper mounting points and, in some case, steering castor.

AERODYNAMIC EFFECTS
Both I.C. and electric buggies go fast enough to be affected by the laws of aerodynamics. Shapes of body shells and the "wings" or "aerofoils" fitted to both can be used to fine tune the buggies' track behaviour.

The biggest effect can be achieved by adjusting the exact position and angle of the rear wing. This is mounted high up

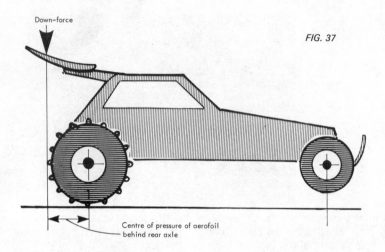

Down-force

FIG. 37

Centre of pressure of aerofoil
behind rear axle

at the rear of the buggy and as its angle is increased, so for any given speed its effect on the weight on the front wheels changes. (See Fig. 37) At high speed the wing has the effect of reducing the power of the steering, making the car easier to drive at high speed. As the car slows down the effect of the wing decreases and the steering starts to bite again. It can be seen that if this is applied with sense then the steering can be set up so that without the effect of the wing, it would be far too powerful at speed. Adjustment is made by either moving the wing backwards and forwards within the limits permitted within the racing rules and by tilting up and down; once again rules limit the extent of adjustment.

FOUR WHEEL STEERING
One of the disadvantages of any four-wheel drive system is that the buggy will have an inherent tendency to under-steer, particularly under power. The latest full-size rally cars with 4WD drive employ torque sharing and multi-ratio coupling between front and rear so that

Twice European 1/8 buggy champion Pedro Martinez flies his Yankee over the bumps.

94

Ball-joint links connect the anti-roll bar to the wishbones in this set-up.

the driver can vary the 4WD effects while on the move. This is more difficult for model buggies and the addition of rear wheel steering is an attempt to overcome this inadequacy.

Inevitably there is greater complication and in the case of I.C. buggies, extra expense, as an extra servo is certainly needed to operate the rear steering. In most cases the proportion of front to rear steering will be advised by the manufacturer and will not seem to be very much. Not very much steering of the rear wheels in in fact necessary or indeed advisable, but with the possibility of steering the rear wheels comes the possibility of altering the toe-in and toe-out of the rear wheels. This does have quite a strong effect and should be experimented with carefully. A little toe-out helps on slippery tracks, while toe-in can be used if there is a lot of grip.

ANTI-ROLL BARS

The anti-roll bar is fitted to increase the roll stiffness of the buggy. The more grip the stiffer the bar can be. If you notice that your buggy lifts a wheel on bends use an anti-roll bar to prevent it. Particularly with a 4WD the idea is to keep all the wheels on the track all of the time, but with very soft suspension with a lot of travel it is not an infrequent situation to find wheels lifting.

CHAPTER 12

Electric Considerations

Advice on how to increase the performance of I.C. buggies was included in Chapter 10 but electric buggies cannot be tuned up quite so easily as their I.C. counterparts. First of all the "fuel supply" or battery pack has a limited capacity and simply putting a more powerful motor in the buggy will make it go faster, yes, but it will probably not run for as long.

Design of electric buggies follows the requirements of competition very closely and competition rules demand that the battery size is limited. There are arguments for and against this. Total removal of control of batteries would result in "money spent" being the performance dictator, whereas at present charging and gear ratio selection skill become the dictators.

Almost the first requirement that electric buggy owners would list would be the possibility of making the buggy run for longer. If the battery is considered as a fuel tank, then it can be seen that it is possible to use it up quickly and go very fast meanwhile, or travel a long way slowly. Motor design, gear ratio choice and driving style and skill affect this.

MOTOR CHOICE
The so-called standard motor is a good starting point, and is limited in specification mainly by price. The armature runs in plain bronze bush bearings, balance is to a reasonable standard and wind of the armature is "mild". This latter factor determines the character of the motor almost more than any other factor. The lower the resistance of the windings on the armature the greater is the potential current flow and thus the greater is the motor power. There are a number of "Buggy Specials" available, and you buy one of these as a step up from the motor supplied with the kit.

"Modified" class motors can vary considerably in specification, with such items as ball-races, diamond trued commutators, dynamic balance and double winds, all of which add to the price, which for racing purposes is limited. In general terms, modified motors will use more current than standard class motors and there is a strong case for the move to use 7 cells for racing in this class, for really a modified motor on 6 cells is not likely to give a very markedly faster run than a standard motor.

This Modified Class motor has ball-races and adjustable timing.

GEAR RATIOS

Whatever motor you choose, the time on the track and the speed will totally depend on the gear ratio chosen. A 'high" ratio means that the motor only turns slowly to make the buggy travel fast, a "low" ratio means that even with the motor rotating very fast indeed, the buggy moves slowly. In practical terms, the bigger (the more teeth) the motor pinion, the higher the ratio. High ratios are chosen to give the buggy a high top speed but, used in the wrong situation, that is on a track with tight bends and short straights, the effect will be to overheat the motor and keep the speed right down.

If the motor is loaded up too much, either by too high a ratio or too much weight, the current consumption will also go up rapidly. The gear ratio must be carefully chosen to allow the motor to "unwind" and not labour. Gear ratios tend to be chosen by reference to running time. As races are run to a length formula, the cars try to cover as many laps of the track as they can in a fixed time, when the ideal situation is one where the battery goes totally flat as the race time limit is reached. If the buggy doesn't complete the race because of the battery going flat before the end, then the standard technique is to fit a smaller motor pinion – lower the ratio. If there is plenty of battery left at the conclusion of the race, then the motor could have been loaded up more so that it used the battery capacity faster. A larger pinion is fitted in this case.

IS THAT ALL?

In very broad terms that is all there is to it, at least from the racing point of view. In very broad terms! Choosing the correct gear ratio is probably the last item on the list, for it may well be that every other single thing about your buggy, charging methods and driving technique are wrong!

Your buggy must be properly set up with really free-moving bearings and a properly run-in motor that is in good condition. Motors will keep on going in very poor condition but will not give good duration or good power. The best motor to use is one with removable brushes; this type of motor lends itself to maintenance so much better, as the brushes are a very critical area.

First step is proper running in, which used to be achieved by simply running the motor for long periods of time without loads, but now "water dipping" is found to give fast and reliable results. The motor is coupled up to a fully charged battery pack and immersed in a bucket of water and run until the first sign of black slurry is seen to come from the motor. The motor is then switched off, allowed to dry out and then lubricated.

Stronger than normal gears in alternative ratios are available from several specialist sources.

Once run in, the motor should be treated with commutator lubricant and have the bearings oiled.

Check that the brushes are not sticking in their holders, as it may be necessary to scrape the sides of them to ease their fit. Feel the springs to check that they are capable of pressing the brushes on to the commutator. Run the motor and press lightly on the brushes in turn to see if there is any improvement in the RPM of the motor if brush pressure is increased. If there is, tweak the brushes to increase the pressure. The magnetism of the ceramic magnets can deteriorate with time and overheating and some motor specialists offer a re-magnetising service that may benefit your motor.

CARING FOR BEARINGS

With a motor that is in top condition, now turn your attention to the rest of the buggy. Clean out all the bearings and check for play. Also make sure that the clearances are right between the gears. The best indication of incorrect clearances is noise — if the gears are noisy, the gear mesh is wrong. The buggy should be almost silent. Re-lubricate using a really good quality oil: not too much, or dirt will be attracted to the moving parts and this will speed up wear. If there are universal joints excessive wear will drain power; there are sometimes tune-up replacement UJs available and these might be more efficient than the standard units. Finally check that excessive play in suspension joints is not allowing the wheels to point in the wrong directions, for too much toe-out or toe-in can be a power sapper.

GOOD CONTACTS

Examine the various connections between battery pack, speed controller and motor to make sure that there are no unnecessary power losses. Clean plugs and sockets, tighten up any screw connectors, check that the wiper on a mechanical speed controller moves fully onto the top speed band.

WEIGH IT UP

Last but by no means least in the search for better performance, consider the weight of your buggy. If it has a resistor speed controller and still carries a receiver battery, then there are obvious areas for weight reduction. At the very least fit a receiver battery eliminator, which will only weigh a few grammes as compared with over 100 grammes for the battery. Don't use the simple diode dropping system, which works satisfactorily on some equipment but can cause mysterious problems with others. It is very cheap, but for the extra cost, a proper transistorised unit is far safer.

Take a look at the amount of wiring there is on your buggy. It is surprising how this adds up to a lot of excess weight as well as extra resistance in the electrical circuit. Beware of spending a lot of time drilling holes in parts to lighten them. Even if you don't weaken the parts a lot, you will have your work cut out to save a lot of weight.

One area that does weigh a lot is waterproofing, particularly the full R/C "crates" that are fitted to some buggies. At the very least, these can be replaced with very light vacuum-formed boxes, but in many instances they can be dispensed with altogether. Most race organisers avoid incorporating any sort of water splash in racing circuits – after all, most people that go racing don't really want to enter waterproofing competitions, they want to race buggies! Unless it is actually raining, there will be little need for waterproofing in its fullest sense. In any event, not everyone wants to keep on running their buggy when it is raining, so splashproofing is all that is really needed.

In the end, the system that provides almost the best waterproofing of all is the lightest imaginable – rubber balloons which are very good, and cheap as well.

Many buggies are supplied with an injection moulded plastic body. This is quite heavy and can easily be replaced with a vacuum-formed polycarbonate

Temporary circuits can be laid out on almost any piece of open ground.

shell body. Such shells are sold as untrimmed and unpainted items which are usually transparent and after trimming to fit the buggy are painted on the inside with special polycarbonate paints.

Using the correct paint is important with this material, as the wrong paint will not stick to the plastic and will in fact attack it, causing it to become brittle and crack up. Trimming can be done with scissors and the edges sanded straight and smooth after rough trimming. Polycarbonate paints can be sprayed or brushed and can even be purchased in aerosol form.

SEVEN CELL RACING

As mentioned at the beginning of this chapter, there is some doubt as to the real worth of racing buggies with modified motors and 6 cells. Quite simply, the $\frac{1}{10}$ buggy is quite heavy and to make it run for 5 minutes plus with a modified motor and 6 cells gives a result which doesn't do justice to the idea of "modified" racing. In other words, it is pointless, as can be demonstrated by the fact that modified races can be won with buggies fitted with standard motors. Add an extra cell and the buggy really does start to take on the feel of a modified car. A big step up in speed is immediately apparent, as long as the dampers are not put on by extending the length of the races.

Most resistor controllers will take 7 cell battery packs but check with the manufacturer of any electronic controller before hooking it up to the extra high voltage pack. Seven cells is not in fact the limit applied by racing rules but is the practical limit for most purposes, enforced by charging limitations. The racing rules allow a maximum of 8 cells but as 8 cell packs are next to impossible to charge with a simple charger from a 12 volt battery, the 7 cell pack seems a favourable compromise. Either special packs can be made up or the extra cell added to the 6 cell pack using extension leads, allowing the possibility of moving the extra cell around the buggy to help achieve the best balance for handling.

Some existing chargers designed for 6 cell packs will charge 7 cell packs, but

Many tune-up accessories are fitted to this basic Tamiya chassis.

the more sophisticated peak voltage sensing types may well refuse to charge the 7 cell pack properly. If it is possible to hook up 18 volts to the charger then this is one solution but it may well be necessary either to have the charger modified or even to purchase a special charger for 7 cell packs.

DRIVING EFFECTS

Just altering driving technique can make all the difference between your buggy running for 5 minutes or 6 minutes. The aim is to drive smoothly, since the heaviest use of current is when the buggy pulls away from rest. It stands to reason that if your buggy is continually spinning out or colliding with obstacles, your racing performance is not going to be too good. It is not so readily appreciated that this will also cut down the duration of the buggy.

The aim should be actually to start from a standstill only once, when the flag drops for the start of the race. If you keep proper watch on the track ahead of your buggy you should be able to slow down in plenty of time and take avoiding action without stopping. If the buggy is properly set up, it will be able to go round corners faster anyway, less power will be used in accelerating up to full speed after each corner and it won't spin out so frequently, once again needing to start from rest.

Nor is it just starting up that uses the juice. If you do see that your buggy is about to spin out, wait until it has actually stopped before using reverse and also has stopped reversing before starting off forward again. Don't use the throttle violently at all. In fact, smooth throttle operation is all a part of smooth driving and will not only pay off in better battery life but will make a surprising difference to the speed at which your buggy laps the track.

APPENDIX 1

1/10 Electric Off-Road Construction Rules

1. APPEARANCE

1.1 Cars entered for off road competitions should be reasonable representations of the style of full size cars generally accepted as being suitable for rally cross, rallying, trail or desert racing.

1.2 Open roll cage style cars will only be permitted to compete if the entrant can supply proof that the car is closely based on a full size example.

1.3 The roll cage of any open roll cage car must enclose all drive and guidance equipment.

1.4 Any commercially available 1/10th scale body shell may be used other than open-wheeled formula 1 type shells or sports racing shells.

1.5 In the case of open cockpit cars a realistic driver figure must be included.

1.6 All cars must make suitable arrangements for racing numbers to be displayed facing to the front and on each side.

1.7 No car may be raced without a body shell being securely fitted at all times.

1.8 When initially entered in a meet the body must be neatly finished.

2. GENERAL CONSTRUCTION RULES

2.1 No car shall be constructed as to be dangerous or damage other competitors' cars.

2.2 A front bumper must be fitted at all times. Any bumper will be made of a resilient material such as rubber or plastic and be a minimum of 2.5mm thick with round edges. Metal bumpers are specifically prohibited. Rear bumpers may be fitted but are not mandatory and must not extend more than four inches past the rear wheel centre.

2.3 Dimensions must conform to the following:
Maximum length – 460mm (including bumpers)
Maximum width – 250mm
Minimum weight – 48oz (1.36Kg) complete and ready to race.

2.4 The chassis can be made of any type of material and can be of any thickness.

2.5 There are no limitations on the steering.

2.6 There are no limitations on the suspension.

2.7 Any type of speed controller may be used but it must be contained within the car and not protrude through the body shell.

2.8 Drive batteries must conform to the following:

The cars will be driven by a maximum of six cells, these cells are sub 'C' cells with a manufacturers' rating of 7.2V. Only cells generally available at a cost not exceeding £3 per cell or £18 per pack of six will be eligible. Entrants must be prepared to open sealed packs on demand of the race scrutineer to demonstrate the eligibility of the cells.

2.9 The Radio box is not mandatory but is recommended.

2.10 There are no limitations on gears.

2.11 Differentials are allowed.

2.12 Ball races may be used.

2.13 Wheels and tyres must conform to the following:

No form of metal or plastic spike tubes or anything similar shall be attached to the tyres. The maximum diameter allowed is 90mm front and rear. Any combination of commercially available wheels and tyres may be used.

2.14 Motors fall into two classes Standard and Modified and must conform to the following:

Standard Class
  i) Only nationally commercially available motors may be used.
  ii) The maximum retail cost of motors not to exceed £10.
  iii) Only unopened, unmodified motors may be used.
  iv) Only one drive motor may be used.

Modified Class
  i) Only motors with a retail cost of £35 and under may be used.
  ii) Only one drive motor may be used.

2.15 Four wheel drive is allowed until such time that the Committee feels a separate class is justified.

3. 380 CLASS

3.1 Rules for the appearance of the 380 class are the same as for the 540 class rules 1.1 to 1.8.

3.2 General construction rules for the 380 class cars are the same as for the 540 class with the following exceptions.
  i) These cars shall be commercially available 380 kits only.
  ii) They can only incorporate the kit supplied chassis.
  iii) Only the ball joints, track rods and servo saver may be altered in the steering equipment.
  iv) The gears may be replaced with stronger alternatives and the ratio altered.
  v) Differentials are not allowed.
  vi) The suspension has to be as per the kit with the additions of dampers only.
  ivii) Only 380S Mabuchi motors are allowed. Maximum retail cost of £6.00.
  viii) Protective covers may be fitted to waterproof the car.

4. R/C EQUIPMENT

4.1 Only legally approved R/C frequencies may be used.

4.2 Entrants should ideally be prepared to use any legal frequency, but in any event should have at least two additional frequencies to that entered available.

4.3 Power Supply for the transmitter must not exceed the designed voltage for the transmitter.

5. TRACK

5.1 Corner cutting must be discouraged by placing markings and barriers.

5.2 Start and finish lines must be marked.

5.3 Track must be at least 6' wide.

5.4 Track should be laid out so that there is no hidden area when viewed from the drivers' rostrum area.

5.5 Adequate protection should be provided for spectators.

5.6 The start area must be a minimum of 10ft. wide.

5.7 All finals must use a grid start based on qualifying, the fastest at the front.

6. RACE PROCEDURES and CHAMPIONSHIP PROCEDURES

6.1 All heats and finals shall be of the same duration.

6.2 Race duration shall be a minimum of five minutes.

6.3 A maximum of two minutes warning will be given prior to the commencement of the race.

6.4 Any car jumping the start signal will be penalised.

6.5 Qualifying heats shall consist of a maximum of ten cars.

6.6 Finals shall consist of a maximum of eight cars.

6.7 There should be a minimum of three qualifying heats per class.

6.8 There will be 5 finals. Open A and Open B with all drivers eligible. The BRCA Championship finals are only open to BRCA members, an 'A' final 20-35% handicap final, and an 0-15% handicap final. (These handicaps are based on the BRCA handicap list.)

6.9 In the 380 class finals there should be two finals, the 'A' final which is open to all and the 0-20% handicap final (if the entry permits) and again the handicap is based on the BRCA handicap list.
Rules 6.8 and 6.9 only apply to points championship meetings.

7. CHAMPIONSHIP POINTS

7.1 The top twenty entrants score points.

7.2 First place scores one point and twentieth place scores twenty points.

7.3 The first eight places are taken from the 'A' final, and ninth to twentieth places are taken on the qualifying positions.

7.4 The number of best scores to count in the calculation of the championship depends upon the number of meetings held and the following formula:
Number of scores to count = Minimum of six or 50% of the listed meetings + 1. (halves rounded down).
e.g. If there are thirteen meetings then $(13 \div 2) + 1 = 7\frac{1}{2}$ which rounded down equals 7.

7.5 The driver with the lowest score wins.

APPENDIX 2

1/8 I.C. Off-Road Construction Rules

1. Aims
To provide a uniform format for ⅛th scale off-road racing cars to compete with one another on an Open National basis. The intention is to encompass all commercially available ⅛ scale cars, yet still encourage invention and innovation with the general aim of developing the hobby by allowing 1-off, home constructed cars, and modifications of kit products.

2. Appearance
i) Cars entered for Off-Road competitions should be reasonable representations of the style of full-size generally accepted as being suitable for Rally Cross, Trial or Desert Racing. A tolerance of 10% in dimensional accuracy is allowable.

ii) Open roll-cage style cars will only be permitted to compete if the entrant can supply proof that the car is closely based on a full size example. The roll-cage of any such car entered must fully enclose all the drive and guidance equipment.

iii) Any commercially available ⅛ scale bodyshell may be used other than open wheeled Formula 1 type and Sports/Racing cars.

iv) In the case of open cockpit cars, a realistic driver figure must be included.

v) All cars must make suitable arrangements for racing numbers to be displayed facing to the front and each side. Cars not displaying clear numbers may not be counted.

vi) No car may be raced without a body shell fitted.

3. Dimensions
Wheelbase:– 270-330mm
Max. Height:– 250mm exc. aerial
Max. Width:– 310mm
Max. Length:– 600mm

Technical Specifications
a) The engine may have a total capacity not exceeding $3.5cm^3$.

b) The fuel tank capacity, including fuel filter + fuel lines up to the carburettor must not exceed $125cm^3$.

c) Tyres must be black except for

sidewall lettering. Diameter min. 75mm, max. 120mm. Max. width 60mm.

d) Rims – fixing bolts or other equipment installed in the wheel rim must not protrude beyond wheel rim. The rim must not extend more than 2mm beyond the exterior of the tyre.

e) At no time will the noise level exceed 80 dB measured at all speeds with the car on the ground measured 10m from the car with the dB meter 1m above the ground.

f) All cars shall have a clutch and brakes such that they be stationary with the engine running.

g) A spoiler made of flexible material is allowed. Max. width 70mm. Max. length 210mm.

h) No part of the chassis may extend beyond the exterior of the body with the exception of the engine and rear axle.

i) Openings in the body must be kept to a minimum, cut-outs are allowed for the following equipment;
    i) cylinder head
    ii) air filter
    iii) fuel filter
    iv) aerial
    v) exhaust pipe
    vi) driver
    vii) roll bar

j) The aerial must be made from a flexible material which will collapse under the weight of an inverted car. Metallic aerials must have the free end protected.

k) A front bumper made of a flexible material not less than 2.5mm thick with corners and sharp edges rounded off must be fitted. This bumper shall not extend more than 50mm beyond the front of the body.

l) Cars must be constructed so as to minimise injury that may result from being hit by a car.

m) A rear bumper made from a flexible material may be fitted.

4. Radio Control Equipment

a) It is the responsibility of each driver to ensure that his equipment does not cause interference to others and that his receiver is not faulty.

b) Only legally approved frequencies are to be used.

c) Driver must be able to provide at least one alternative frequency.

d) Flags shall not be used on aerials during races.

e) A frequency "peg board" system shall be used at all times.

f) Under no circumstances shall a transmitter be taken on to the track.

g) All frequency changes must be approved by the Race Director.

h) Additional batteries designed to increase the transmitter voltage may not be used.

5. Scrutineering

a) Only cars which conform to the construction rules may compete.

b) Only one entry per driver will be accepted.

c) Cars may be inspected at any time during the race and after the final.

d) Any part of the car may be substituted during a race, except the chassis or chassis rails, the chassis or chassis rails may be changed with the approval of the race director.

e) Damage caused during a race will not be penalised except in the case of excessive noise from the engine or the total loss of the body.

6. Concours D'Elegance
a) A Concours may be held before the start of racing.
b) The body and chassis of cars judged for Concours must take part in the race.
c) The Concours judge may if he wishes take into account the chassis preparation.

7. Entrance Requirements
a) Entry forms for BRCA Championship Meetings should be distributed via Circuit Chatter.
b) Closing date for entries should not be more than 10 days before the race.
c) In the event of over-subscription of a meeting the organiser shall accept entries in the order in which he receives them, using the post mark as the date of entry.
d) The organiser should appoint the following officials.
i) Race Director – in control of all racing.
ii) Referee – in control of driving standards, interference decisions, protests, rule application etc., scrutineering.
iii) Chief Timekeeper – in control of timekeeping.
e) Entrants should be required to provide proof of BRCA membership.
f) In the case of late arrival to a

race, all properly entered drivers will be accepted until the end of qualifying heats.

8. Race Procedure
a) A drivers' briefing must be held by the Race Director, Referee and Timekeeper before racing starts.
b) The drivers' briefing should include guidance on the following:
i) Starts and Finish.
ii) Refuelling, marshalling, repairs, transmitters.
iii) Protest procedure.
iv) Drivers' conduct.
c) All drivers shall have a minimum of 3 qualifying heats of 8-15 minutes duration.
d) A maximum number of 8 cars per qualifying heat.
e) Qualification for finals shall be determined by each driver's single best heat time. In the event of a tie, the second best heat time shall be used.
f) There shall be a period of 3 minutes from the finish of a heat to the start of the following heat. An audible warning shall be given 1 minute before the start of all heats.

9. Start Procedure
a) At the start of all races, all cars are to be held on the start line by the mechanics.
b) The starter shall indicate to the mechanics to release the cars and step back 1 pace, and all cars shall remain stationary. On the starter raising his flag, the race shall then start.
c) The starter shall hold cars stationary at the start for a maximum of 10 seconds.

d) Any car which moves forward before the starter raises his flag may be subject to a penalty.

e) The starter may call a re-start if he cannot identify the car(s) that made a false start.

10. Finish

a) A car will be deemed to have finished the race the first time it crosses the finish line after the expiry of the duration of any heat or final.

b) Only cars on the track at the time of the finish shall be given a split time, i.e. the total laps completed at the finish shall be the time, with no time for last lap.

c) No car may be pushed over the finish line.

11. Race Interruption

a) The Race Director may decide to interrupt the race due to rain.

b) If all competitors have not had one heat in the dry but all have had one in the wet, only the wet heat results will be counted.

c) If more than half the final has been run and the race has to be stopped the positions at the time of interruption will be the result.

d) In the case of a heat being interrupted the entire heat will be re-run.

12. Protests

a) The organiser may correct anything deemed necessary without a protest.

b) All protests must be made in writing to the referee, together with a £10 deposit. If the protest is upheld this money will be re-imbursed.

c) Protests must be made within 5 minutes of the results in question.

d) Protests regarding the legality of cars must be made in writing together with the fee to the referee.

13. Penalties and Black Flag

a) The Race Director may at his discretion penalise competitors by disqualification or loss or best heat time for the following infringements:

i. Disregard of official decisions.

ii. Corner cutting.

iii. Unauthorised use of transmitters.

iv. Incorrect use of pits.

v. Repairs or refuelling on the track.

vi. Unauthorised frequency changes. Illegal frequencies.

vii. Unauthorised changing of chassis plate/rails.

viii. Cars not conforming to regulations.

ix. Non-sporting behaviour, bad language.

b) A car which is black flagged must be removed from the track immediately.

A car may be black flagged for the following infringements:

i. Deliberately impeding the progress of other cars.

ii. Non-sporting racing.

iii. Driving in a dangerous manner.

iv. Cars in an undriveable or dangerous condition. (These cars may restart after repairs, with the Race Director's/referee's permission).

v. Cars losing their bodies or whose silencers become in-

A jump adds excitement to the racing.

effective (These cars may re-start after the necessary re-pairs).

14. Finals and National Championship Series

a) There shall be two National Championships run con-currently.

i. Restricted – open only to cars with 1 pair of driven wheels.

ii. Unrestricted – open to cars with any number of driven wheels.

b) There will be no discrimination between Restricted and Unre-stricted entries; both are of equal status and will run to-gether in qualifying heats.

c) Two finals will be run of 20-30 minutes duration, one for Re-stricted Classes and the other for Unrestricted.

d) These finals shall alternate in programme position through the Championship series.

e) Depending on the number of entries the organisers may put on A, B, (and C) finals.

15. Finals Qualification

a) At the termination of the quali-fying rounds the top 16 quali-fiers overall, irrespective of class, shall be placed in order.

b) Any driver of a Restricted car placing in the top 8 qualifiers shall be given the option to drive in either the Restricted or Unrestricted final in order of qualifying.

c) In the event of high qualifying Restricted drivers opting to run in the Restricted Final, the Unrestricted Final shall be made up to 8 cars by the inclusion of the lowest qualifying Restricted cars.

d) Points will be awarded to drivers in both Restricted and Unrestricted classes on the following basis:

1st	21 points	3rd	18
2nd	19	4th	17
5th	16	7th	14
6th	15	8th	13

Down to 20th place – 1 point.

e) In the case of both Restricted and Unrestricted Finals a "Le Mans" style start should be used. Cars will be placed in echelon on the side of the track furthest from the drivers' rostrum not less than 1.5 metres apart and not more than 2.5 metres apart. Boxes shall be indicated by some suitable means and cars placed in order of qualification, the fastest car at the front of the grid.

f) Team selection for International events shall be made on the basis of the BRCA Championship series results. Restricted and Unrestricted points scores will be amalgamated into one single table and offers of team places will be made in order of precedence on the list.

In the event of refusal of the offer of a place, the next person on the list will be offered the place.

g) Commemorative plaques or trophies may be awarded to event winners. No cash prizes or goods shall be awarded. A perennial trophy will be awarded to both the Restricted and Unrestricted Champion.

16. Track and Safety

a) Spectators and marshalls should be protected from the risk of being hit by cars.

b) Track markers should be such that they minimise the risks of cars becoming airborne.

c) Track markers and tracks should be designed so as to minimise risk of damage to cars.

APPENDIX 3

Useful Addresses

Model Cars magazine,
P.O. Box 35,
Wolsey House,
Wolsey Road,
Hemel Hempstead,
Herts.
HP2 4SS

British Radio Car Association,
6 Queensway,
Queensbury,
Bradford,
W. Yorks.

M.A.P. (Insurance)
(See Model Cars above for address)

Pick-up truck bodies are a popular choice, as exemplified by this 4-wheel drive Tamiya.